# The English Civil Wars

## A Beginner's Guide

D0953928

**ONEWORLD BEGINNER'S GUIDES** combine an original, inventive, and engaging approach with expert analysis on subjects ranging from art and history to religion and politics, and everything in-between. Innovative and affordable, books in the series are perfect for anyone curious about the way the world works and the big ideas of our time.

# The English Civil Wars

## A Beginner's Guide

Patrick Little

ONEWORLD

A Oneworld Paperback Original

Published in North America, Great Britain and Australia
by Oneworld Publications, 2014

Copyright © Patrick Little 2014

The moral right of Patrick Little to be identified as the Author
of this work has been asserted by him/her in accordance with
the Copyright, Designs and Patents Act 1988

All rights reserved
Copyright under Berne Convention
A CIP record for this title is available
from the British Library

ISBN 9781780743318
eISBN 9781780743325

Typeset by Siliconchips Services Ltd, UK
Printed and bound in Denmark by
Nørhaven A/S

Oneworld Publications
10 Bloomsbury Street
London WC1B 3SR
England

Stay up to date with the latest books,
special offers, and exclusive content from
Oneworld with our monthly newsletter

Sign up on our website
**www.oneworld-publications.com**

# Contents

# Preface

In writing this book, I had two primary aims. The first was to produce a concise, accessible account of the conflicts collectively known as the English Civil Wars. The second was to try to give the reader some idea of what it was like to live through that traumatic episode. These aims explain the structure of what follows, which falls into two parts: a narrative of events between the outbreak of war in 1642 and the final defeat of the royalists at Worcester in 1651; and a thematic study of the military, religious, political, and social aspects of the civil war period.

This book has been informed by my own experiences in trying to bring the period to a wider audience. I am grateful to various groups and individuals for encouraging me to continue with what some colleagues may consider a quixotic venture. First, I am indebted to the late Professor Barry Coward, who involved me in teaching mature students at Birkbeck College, London, and then introduced me to The Cromwell Association. More recently, my role as chairman of the latter has allowed me to make contact with a wide range of groups catering for enthusiasts for the period, especially the Battlefields Trust, the Naseby Project, the John Hampden Society, the English Civil War Society, and the Sealed Knot. Parts of this book originated as a talk given to the 'Marston Moor Live' event staged in July 2011 and hosted by Jo and David Smakman at Marston Grange. I am very grateful to them, and to audiences drawn from a variety of organizations, for their helpful comments and encouragement. My thanks also to Lilian Ladle and her team for discussion of the excavations at Bestwall near Wareham in Dorset, and to Dr Kerry Houston for information on John Oker. Dr David L. Smith, who kindly read a draft of the manuscript, provided valuable comments and criticisms. My wife, Susanne, also read the text, and drew my attention to various places where more explanation and clarification were badly needed.

Inevitably, I have relied heavily on the work of many historians, past and present. As this series does not include notes, I must beg indulgence from those whose work I have used and yet cannot acknowledge in the usual way. The guide to further reading at the end of the book includes those books and articles that I found most useful, and others that will help the reader to explore in greater depth for him- or herself.

Finally, I would like to thank my family for their support and encouragement; and on this occasion especially my sister, Clare, to whom this book is dedicated.

The English Civil Wars

1642-1651

# 1

# The outbreak of war

In the early afternoon of 23 October 1642, the armies of King Charles I and his parliament stood facing each other at Edgehill in Warwickshire. The king's forces, around 12,000 strong, were positioned on the slopes of the Edgehill escarpment – a long 300-foot-high ridge that dominated the surrounding area. Parliament's army, roughly the same size as that of the king, and led by the newly appointed 'lord general', the earl of Essex, had formed up in front of the village of Kineton. A wide-open area, known as the 'great meadow', separated the two armies.

Despite the rolling drums, the boldly displayed flags, and the shouted encouragements from officers to their men, the prevailing mood was one of doubt. The king's men were keen to defeat the 'rebels' in one decisive encounter, and to march on London to dictate peace terms, but there had been disputes among the high command in the hours before the battle started. The king's general of foot, the earl of Lindsey, had complained of being slighted. The decision to fight at Edgehill had been taken 'without advising with him', he complained, and the army's deployment on the battlefield had been 'in a form that he liked not'. Lindsey felt his honour was at stake, and resigned his command, returning to his own foot regiment in the front line.

Parliament's commanders had problems of their own. They were well aware of the risks they were taking, leading an armed revolt against their lawful king. Essex knew that he could follow his father, Elizabeth's favourite, the 2nd earl, to the block. His concern for his position – and that of all his friends and comrades – may have been a factor in his decision to fight a defensive battle. He did not intend to become famous as the man who had attacked his sovereign. Junior officers shared this sense of revulsion at what was about to take place, and at the very start of the battle one of the parliamentarian cavalry officers, Sir Faithful Fortescue, led his troop from the parliamentarian lines to join the king's side.

There was also some doubt as to the quality of the forces that had been raised hastily in the previous few weeks. As Oliver Cromwell, then a parliamentarian captain, remembered telling John Hampden after the battle: 'Your troopers…are most of them old decayed servingmen and tapsters and such kind of fellows, and, said I, their troopers are gentlemen's sons, younger sons and persons of quality; do you think that the spirits of such base and mean fellows will be ever able to encounter gentlemen that have honour and courage and resolution in them?' Nor was Parliament's army the only one to feel anxiety at the poor quality of its recruits. The decision to use a simplified battle order – one of the issues that had so offended the earl of Lindsey – was probably taken because of the lack of muskets in the ranks of the king's army. Some of the royalists were armed with only agricultural implements and cudgels. It was painfully apparent to both sides that they were amateurs, who were being forced to fight if not against their wills, then against their better judgement. One can guess the questions that ran through the minds of the combatants as the drums sounded the advance. Could the peace-loving English really be fighting one another? Why had Parliament and the king not been able to settle their differences by peaceful means? Was the world being turned upside-down? In order to appreciate the causes of the conflict that broke out in the summer of 1642, we must look at the two most important areas of dispute: politics and religion.

# A political crisis?

England in the seventeenth century was a deeply conservative place, with a rigid social and political hierarchy. One reason for this was that the 'political nation' – the group of people who had some stake in how decisions were made – was relatively sizeable. In countries like France or Spain, which were large and diverse, containing numerous semi-autonomous regions with their own systems of law, government and taxation, royal authority was exercised by crown officials, or delegated to great noblemen subject to, or allied with, the ruling dynasty. Except in cities, where urban elites had some degree of self-government, the European 'lower orders' had no say at all in how they were governed, or taxed. England was different. There, the king's power was not based on magnates or bureaucrats, but on a host of volunteers, working within a fairly uniform system that covered the whole country: these included the MPs and peers who gathered in Parliament to pass laws and vote in taxes; a similar group in the shires who served as justices of the peace (JPs), deputy lieutenants, or commissioners; and, on a parish level, the lesser men who were constables, jurors, or churchwardens. The theory that society was a pyramid, with the king at its apex, was reflected in reality. All power, whether legal, military, economic, or religious, derived ultimately from the crown, and most of England was subject to, and accepting of, this stable political system.

There was, however, an important caveat. For the government to run smoothly, all these local men had to be willing to serve, unpaid; and this willingness depended on whether they thought they had a chance of influencing policy, on whatever level, and whether the king had the best interests of the nation at heart. Under James I, the system had worked fairly well, and the king had been careful to remain flexible, to modify or reverse unpopular decisions, and to smooth ruffled feathers. Charles I was not made in his father's image. Encouraged by those who saw the monarch as enjoying 'divine right' to rule – being answerable not to his people but to God alone – Charles was extremely reluctant to compromise with his subjects. He was also a man who loved order and decorum, who restricted access to himself through a formal court, and who reacted very badly to being opposed. Serious opposition only provoked Charles to retaliate, seeking to undermine opponents, to court his enemies' enemies – and that made him appear untrustworthy and duplicitous.

The crown may have been the ultimate source of authority, but it was not the only focus for political activity. At each

## CHARLES I AND HENRIETTA MARIA

Historians have tended to be quite rude about Charles I. He is compared unfavourably with his canny father, and his main feature – before and during the civil wars – is often said to be inflexibility. He was a man who found compromise difficult, who tended to stand on his honour, and make extreme pronouncements that allowed no room for manoeuvre. Nor did Charles consider himself bound by agreements – especially those made under duress. It was hardly surprising he came to a sticky end in 1649. There is much truth in this, but there is also another side of Charles I. He was a connoisseur who collected paintings and other works of fine art – today's royal collection is founded on his purchases. He was certainly sincere in his religious beliefs, and in his desire to see a stronger, richer church. In addition, he more than fulfilled the first duty of any sovereign – the production of an heir. Seven of his children survived him, including three sons: Charles, prince of Wales (later Charles II), James, duke of York (later James II), and Henry, duke of Gloucester.

Charles's wife, the French princess Henrietta Maria, was a strong character, never far from controversy. During the 1630s, she established a lavish chapel at Somerset House, which became the focus for Catholics at court, and during the civil wars she raised money for the royalists' cause on the continent, and attempted to persuade the French to intervene on the king's side. As a widow, she looked back on her early years as queen with great affection: 'I was the happiest and most fortunate of queens, for not only had I every pleasure the heart could desire, I had a husband who adored me'.

level of the political hierarchy, whether at the quarter sessions held by JPs, or the gentry meeting at the mustering of the local trained bands, there was the opportunity for discussion, and dissent. This was most apparent in Parliament. Parliament, made up of the House of Lords (with lay peers and bishops) and the House of Commons (with representatives from the shires and the boroughs), was not organized along 'party' lines, although MPs could align themselves into factions on particular issues. Rather, each MP and peer was influenced by an array of personal, family, local, regional, and religious factors. Under Elizabeth I and James I, it had been possible for the crown to guide and channel debate and legislation, working through the government officials and courtiers who sat in both Houses. Parliament already had a highly developed sense of its own privileges, its rights and powers, that a sensible monarch was careful to respect; and, as the representative of the 'political nation', Parliament also reflected the concerns that crown policy raised throughout the country.

It was hardly surprising that an imperious, inflexible king like Charles I would find Parliament difficult to handle. Charles had first fallen out with his parliaments in the 1620s, when an unpopular foreign policy – which combined a refusal to support the Protestant states in Europe with ineffectual naval expeditions against France and Spain – led to Parliament withholding taxation. He had responded by raising money without consent. Many MPs had also opposed the king's religious policies, which were seen by many as undermining the Protestant settlement, and even as ushering in Roman Catholicism. Charles's reaction was not to address the complaints, but to silence the complainers. In 1629, he refused to call any more sessions of Parliament, and embarked instead on a period known as the 'personal rule'. The next eleven years until 1640 thus saw a distancing of Charles and his subjects, made worse by his insistence on using his own powers to raise money, notably 'ship money', which maintained the navy. Levying taxes without Parliament's agreement raised fears

**Figure 1** Charles I. Portrait by Anthony van Dyck c 1636.

of 'arbitrary rule' – the contemporary term for the sort of royal absolutism seen in Catholic Europe. Charles did not debate with those who refused to pay; he pursued them through the courts in a series of notorious test cases. With their rights trampled on, and no prospect of presenting their grievances through Parliament, the volunteers who operated local government began to feel alienated.

Further problems were created by unrest in Scotland. The northern kingdom was united to England only through the monarch – when James VI of Scotland became James I of England in 1603 – and it had its own parliament, legal system, and church government. It was the last of these that would cause Charles I the most difficulty, as he tried to force the Presbyterian Scots to accept a prayer book similar to that in England in 1637. Rebellion against the king's religious policies in Scotland in 1638 led to the raising of an English army to march north in 1639. Peace was negotiated before there was any bloodshed, but the main issue had not been solved.

Charles began preparing for another campaign against his unruly subjects in the north. A new army could not be funded without Parliament voting to provide the money, so in the spring of 1640 Charles had to call the Short Parliament – so-called because it was soon dissolved in disarray, as Charles realized that a grant of money would only be agreed if grievances were addressed. An attempt to fight a new war with the Scots in the summer brought defeat and humiliation. Without the means to pay off the Scots (who occupied northern England), Charles had no choice but to call the Long Parliament in November. For the next nine months, the king was forced to look on, impotent, as his opponents in the two Houses gleefully brought down his chief advisers and reversed many of his most prized policies.

Charles had given ground, but he had done so with bad grace. The key issue over the next year was that of trust. Charles was eager to turn the tables on his enemies, and became involved in ill-advised ventures in order to do so. In the spring of 1641, he sponsored a plot within the army to stage a coup in London against his enemies in Parliament; and, in the autumn, he was implicated in another plot to seize his chief opponents in Scotland.

Both schemes served to shake any faith his opponents may have had in his willingness to reform.

However, it was the outbreak of rebellion by the Catholics of Ireland in October 1641 that did Charles the most damage. Like Scotland, Ireland was in theory united to England only through the king, but the island had for a long time been treated as subordinate by its larger neighbour, and this attitude was strengthened by the century-old policy of removing Irish landowners and 'planting' their lands with settlers from England (and, from 1603, from Scotland as well). This inevitably led to tensions, made worse by the Irish adherence to the Roman Catholic Church, and a general economic crisis, which many blamed on the Dublin government. The rebellion in 1641 brought attacks on the settler population, and soon the stories of massacres of innocent Protestants by bloodthirsty Catholics reached England.

There is no evidence that Charles had anything to do with the Irish rebellion, but his opponents in Parliament were ready to link it to existing fears that the king secretly planned to introduce Catholicism and arbitrary government in England. Charles, under pressure, tried another coup. On 4 January 1642, he arrived at the Commons with soldiers, to arrest the 'five members' – the ringleaders of the opposition – John Pym, John Hampden, Denzil Holles, William Strode, and Sir Arthur Hesilrige, alongside a prominent peer, Lord Mandeville. The hostile reaction from Parliament and the citizens of London shocked the king, who withdrew to Hampton Court on 10 January, fearing for his safety.

In the following months, Parliament insisted on raising troops to defeat the rebellion in Ireland, but the king, who suspected these troops would be used against him in England, refused to give his assent to the necessary bill. In March, Parliament instead passed a militia ordinance (a measure that did not require the king's agreement) and proceeded to appoint its own lords lieutenant and lords deputy in the English counties. The political unity, the accepted hierarchy, that had characterized English society only a few months before, had started to unravel. Trust, on which the whole system depended, had begun to evaporate.

In June, Parliament's 'Nineteen Propositions' presented the king with an ultimatum. If he agreed to give Parliament a role in the appointment of officers of state and the reform of religion; if regular Parliaments were guaranteed and the militia ordinance accepted as law; and if there were harsh measures against Catholics at home and abroad, then conflict could be averted. The king rejected these terms out of hand on 18 June, and both sides prepared for war.

One of the greatest conundrums of 1642 is how Charles I managed to attract sufficient support to field an army in the first place. At the opening of the Long Parliament, the king was almost completely isolated – especially once his closest advisers and officials had been imprisoned or forced to flee – and Parliament was more or less united in its opposition to his policies. Yet, by the summer of 1642, large areas of the country supported him, as did many peers and gentry, and a surprising number of his erstwhile critics had become his friends.

The sudden growth of a royalist party was in large part a result of the increasing confidence and ambition of the king's opponents at Westminster. Not content with reversing the worst of Charles's policies and removing his chief advisers, MPs and peers had sought to prune royal power still further and, above all, to press for religious changes that would have made the old church unrecognizable. The reaction could be seen from the summer of 1641, when various MPs objected to what was happening, and especially in the spring of 1642, when Parliament overreached itself by trying to raise troops without royal authority, through the militia ordinance. The tone, as well as the contents, of the Nineteen Propositions justified such concerns. Just as Parliament proclaimed that its rebellion was in the true interests of king and kingdom, so the thousand royalists who joined Charles when he raised his standard at Nottingham in August 1642 saw themselves

## THE ENGLISH CIVIL WAR?

The conflict between 1642 and 1651 is generally known as the English Civil War, but this title raises two problems. First, there were three different wars during the period 1642–51. The first civil war (1642–6) ended with the defeat of Charles I and the surrender of his capital, Oxford. The second civil war (1648) was shorter and more diffuse, comprising a series of uprisings in Kent and Essex, South Wales, the south-west and north-west, supported by an invasion of northern England by the Scots in support of Charles I. The third civil war consisted of only one campaign – that brought another Scottish army marching down the west of England, to be defeated by Cromwell at Worcester in September 1651. The second problem is that the 'English Civil War' was not only an English war. Charles I was heavily reliant on Welsh soldiers, especially when forming his infantry regiments, and the Scots were involved in the wars from 1644 to 1646 on the side of Parliament, and in 1648 and 1651 in support of Charles I and Charles II. Events in England were also strongly influenced by a major rebellion and protracted war in Ireland, which broke out in October 1641 and continued until the last pockets of resistance were stamped out by Cromwell's army in 1653. Aspects of what some have termed 'the war of the three kingdoms' or 'the British civil wars' will inevitably appear in this book, even though the primary focus is on England.

as defending the monarchy against those who wanted to change England for the worse. And there were many others who agreed with them. As a result, on 23 October, Charles was able to muster a substantial army on the slopes of Edgehill.

# A war of religion?

When considering the political causes of the civil wars, it was necessary to go back fifteen years or so, to the beginning of the reign of Charles I. The religious causes originated over a hundred years earlier, during the reign of Charles's great-great-uncle, Henry VIII. The Reformation of the 1530s had created a Church of England that sat awkwardly between the reformed churches of the continent and the Catholic Church of Rome. In time, this Anglican *via media* (or middle way) came to be seen as a great boon, allowing the English church to avoid the excesses of its rivals, but its hybrid form had many contradictions. For example, the theology of the new church was similar to that of John Calvin's reformed church in Geneva, but in the Book of Common Prayer it retained a liturgy that was basically Roman Catholic, and the church continued to be governed by the old system, presided over by bishops. As a result, there were some within the church who hoped for further development, especially the so-called 'puritans', who sought to bring it closer to the reformed churches of Europe and were suspicious of ceremonies and vestments that smacked too much of Rome. In the early seventeenth century, few puritans refused to attend their parish churches – they were content to push for reform from within, and in the meantime to conduct their own prayer meetings and Bible studies at home, while seeking out approved preachers when they could. As Joseph Bentham, vicar of Boughton in Northamptonshire, put it, the puritans were merely 'practising Protestants; such men who daily read the scriptures, pray with their families, teach them the way to heaven'.

This broad, 'national church', accepted by most of the people and with common forms of worship and doctrine, was fostered by James I, but it was destabilized by Charles I, who promoted a group of clergy that became known as the 'Laudians'. These Laudians were influenced by the writings of the Dutch theologian Arminius, who questioned the church's Calvinist theology and put much more emphasis on the sacraments (Baptism and Holy Communion) than on preaching as the means to receive Grace from God. Initially championed by Richard Neile, bishop of Durham in the 1620s, the Laudians took control of the church with the appointment of William Laud as archbishop of Canterbury in 1633. With their emphasis on church services

## PURITANS, LAUDIANS, AND ANGLICANS?

The words used to describe different religious groups and persuasions are also problematic. 'Puritan' was a term of abuse for those who sought to 'purify' the church in the late sixteenth and early seventeenth centuries – the supporters of such reforms called themselves 'the godly' or 'the saints'. The term 'Laudian' for those who backed the high church reforms associated with Archbishop Laud is not ideal either, as it ignores those, such as Bishop Neile of Durham, who fostered similar ideas in the decades before Laud became all powerful. Nor is the word 'Anglican' for mainstream members of the Church of England very useful, as it only entered common parlance after the Restoration. With all these terms, there is also the underlying problem of lumping together men and women of rather different views into groups that suggest a greater coherence than they actually had – a false notion of religious 'parties' or even fixed denominations. Having said that, these names are familiar, and require little further explanation; they also reflect a view at the time, that such groups *were* organized and coherent, and these perceptions were important in shaping the religious disputes of the period. The alternatives are not obvious, and so the traditional terms have been used, with some reluctance, in this book.

(using the set forms of the Book of Common Prayer) and especially Holy Communion, the Laudians were determined to make churches holy places rather than rooms for preaching. This desire to re-establish 'the beauty of holiness' led to the introduction of artwork into churches and cathedrals, choirs and organs, the use of elaborate ceremonies, and, above all, a renewed reverence to the communion table, now termed an 'altar', which was placed at the far east end of the church, rather than in the midst of the congregation.

Although Laudianism gained some support from their congregations, who welcomed the greater sense of reverence, and the chance to repair and beautify neglected churches, it also provoked the puritan element within the church, who could not tolerate what they saw as a blatant attempt to bring the Church of England closer to Rome. Written attacks on Laud and his clergy by Henry Burton, John Bastwick, William Prynne, and others led to harsh measures against them through the civil and church courts, while the refusal of others to comply with strictures brought the removal of puritan ministers and the prosecution of lay offenders in the dioceses.

When the Caroline regime began to fall apart (thanks in large part to the rebellion of the Presbyterian Scots) and Parliament was recalled in 1640, the political nation was more or less united in its opposition to Laudianism, with future royalists also calling for the reform of the church. When the puritan MP Harbottle Grimston denounced Laud as 'the sty of all pestilential filth', and compared him to 'a busy angry wasp, his sting is in the tail of everything', his views would have been echoed by many conformist Anglicans. Retribution was swift. Laud was imprisoned, along with the most notorious of his bishops, and innovations in religion were reversed; the victims of the Laudians, seen as martyrs, were compensated; and by the summer of 1641 it seemed that a return to the Jacobean consensus was the most likely outcome. Over the next twelve months, however, such hopes faded. The puritans, not content with returning to the status quo, now took the opportunity to push further, demanding the removal of bishops, the abolition of the Prayer Book, and a church settlement more like that of Geneva than Canterbury.

The prospect of cleansing the church and returning to the good old days of Elizabeth and James had been welcomed by many church-goers, who found the Laudian innovations unpalatable; but the 'root and branch' reforms demanded by the radicals during 1641 went much too far for the average Anglican. During the winter of 1641–2, there was a series of petitions from English counties calling for the church to be protected against the puritans. The Cheshire petition, subscribed by 9,000 people, emphasized the strength of feeling in the county for 'our pious, laudable and ancient form of divine service' according to the Book of Common Prayer, adding that there was 'scarce any family or person that can read, but are furnished with the Books of

**Figure 2**   Henrietta Maria of France. Portrait by Anthony van Dyck c 1637.

Common Prayer; in the conscionable use whereof many Christian hearts have found unspeakable joy and comfort'.

This backlash was of tremendous importance in providing the king with the support that he needed to resist Parliament by force in 1642. The leaching of support from Parliament in turn encouraged Charles's critics to dig in. The king's hostility to the Presbyterian Scots, the outbreak of rebellion by the Irish Catholics in October 1641, and the increasing importance of the Catholic queen, Henrietta Maria, in Charles's counsels further encouraged the parliamentarians in their distrust of the king, and made open rebellion seem the only option. As Parliament told the Scottish government in early September, their 'chiefest aim' was 'the truth and purity of the reformed religion, not only against popery but against all other superstitious sects and innovations whatsoever'.

## England divided

In simple terms, the outbreak of the English Civil War was caused by a short-term political crisis, and a long-term religious problem of gradually increasing intensity. It was only when the two coincided – largely thanks to the failings of Charles I as king – that the conditions for civil war were created. It should be reiterated that, for both Charles's supporters and his critics, civil war was not a welcome choice. There were a few 'fiery spirits' on both sides who thought that a single decisive battle would accomplish what months of arguing had not; but for the majority of the country, from the leading politicians and generals to the ordinary townspeople and peasants, civil war was a complete failure, a breakdown in the stable, consensual society that was highly valued, not least as the Thirty Years War raging across Germany provided a terrible example of what could happen when a country fell victim to prolonged warfare. This, in part, explains why the early course of the war was so hesitant, with repeated attempts to make peace, and many doing their best to remain neutral.

In the days before Edgehill, the royalist Sir Edmund Verney said that 'I do not like the quarrel, and do heartily wish that the king would yield and consent to what they desire; so that my conscience is only concerned in honour and gratitude to follow my master'. A few months later, Verney's words were to be echoed by the parliamentarian general Sir William Waller, when he wrote, 'that great God, which is the searcher of my heart,

## ROUNDHEADS AND CAVALIERS?

The traditional view of the civil wars is not much different from that caricatured in W.C. Sellar and R.J. Yeatman's *1066 and All That*: 'Charles I was a Cavalier King and therefore had a small pointed beard, long flowing curls, a large, flat, flowing hat, and *gay attire*. The Roundheads, on the other hand, were clean-shaven and wore tall, conical hats, white ties, and *sombre garments*. Under these circumstances, a Civil War was inevitable.'

This is all wrong. First, while a few extreme puritans objected to sumptuous clothes as nothing but vanity, in general the clothing worn by either side in the civil wars was almost identical – as can be seen in the flamboyant portraits of many of the leading parliamentarian politicians and soldiers. Second, 'Cavalier' – a term meaning horseman – was almost as derogatory as 'Roundhead' – derived from the custom of London apprentices having closely cropped heads. Finally, the popular image of the dashing Cavalier as opposed to the dour Roundhead reinforces a stereotype of the civil war as some kind of class conflict that is most unhelpful when exploring the complexities of the period. 'Royalist' and 'parliamentarian', straightforward and self-explanatory contemporary terms, are surely preferable.

knows with what a sad sense I go upon this service, and with what a perfect hatred I detest this war without an enemy'. It is to this sad conflict that we now turn.

# 2

# 'This war without an enemy': the first civil war, 1642–6

## Opening stages, 1642–3

The battle of Edgehill ended in stalemate. The royalist cavalry had swept away the opposing parliamentarian horse troops, but by following them off the field had also removed the king's best hope of victory. The infantry had slugged it out until both sides were exhausted, and as night fell neither side had gained any real advantage. The next day, both armies withdrew, with the earl of Essex taking his men back to Warwick, leaving the road to London open to the royalists.

Instead of seizing the opportunity by striking at the undefended capital, Charles marched his army slowly eastwards, occupying Oxford (which became his headquarters) and inching down the Thames Valley to Reading. Parliament, despondent that they had not won a quick victory, tried to open peace negotiations, but to no avail.

By the time the king's nephew, Prince Rupert, had persuaded his uncle to attack London, Essex's army had returned to the capital, and the city's trained bands mobilized. The prince overran an outpost at Brentford on 12 November. In response, Essex mustered a large force at Turnham Green, blocking the road to London. Rather than risk a fight on disadvantageous ground, the king withdrew and reached Oxford once again by the end of

November. As winter set in, it was clear that the main armies on both sides had achieved remarkably little.

The war in the regions had been no more decisive. Parliament had established garrisons in most of the major ports, from Bristol and Plymouth to Dover and Hull, thanks to its control of the navy. In the north, the parliamentarian commander, Lord Fairfax, and his son, Sir Thomas, played a game of cat and mouse with the superior forces of the king, under the earl of Newcastle. In the south-west, the Cornish army under Sir Ralph Hopton sparred with the Devon parliamentarians, with neither side able to make inroads across the Tamar. An even more fluid picture emerges in the south, the midlands, and the Welsh marches, where rival groups of gentlemen tried to secure local towns and cities and to wrest control of castles and country houses from each other. At this stage, only a minority of landowners were actively engaged for either side, with the majority trying to keep out of trouble. Neutralist pacts were attempted – much to the alarm of those at Westminster or Oxford – in Yorkshire and the south-west during the winter of 1642–3.

## 'ESSEX THE REBEL'

Born in 1591, Robert Devereux, 3rd earl of Essex, came from a distinguished family beset with troubles. His father, the 2nd earl, Elizabeth I's last favourite, was executed after plotting against the queen in 1601, and his mother remarried and moved to Ireland, leaving the young earl to be brought up by strangers. He was rehabilitated by James I but never settled at court, and his reputation suffered from two failed marriages – one ended in divorce, the other in estrangement – and the failure to produce a son and heir. Essex served in the Thirty Years War in the early 1620s, and was one of the commanders of the disastrous expedition against the Spanish port of Cadiz in 1625. Estranged from the court thereafter, he became a leading critic of the crown during the Long Parliament, and an obvious – and popular – candidate as Parliament's lord general in 1642. Whether his pre-civil war experiences made him a cautious and reactive commander during the civil war is uncertain, but they probably contributed to his prickliness and obsession with his own honour. The royalist press needled him mercilessly, dubbing him 'The Great Cuckold' and 'Ramhead', with reference to the infidelity of his wives. Essex's military career was not wildly successful, but he was loved by his men, and his personal standing in Parliament was second to none before his disastrous defeat at Lostwithiel in August 1644. Essex died of a stroke in September 1646, and he was given a lavish funeral.

This desire to bring the hostilities to a rapid end also pervaded the Houses of Parliament. The failure of the Edgehill campaign had led to division between those who called for peace on almost any terms, led by the earl of Northumberland in the Lords and Denzil Holles in the Commons, and the more radical opponents of Charles I, such as John Pym and Viscount Saye, whose attacks on the king and his policies before the war had made them hate figures at Oxford. This 'war party' feared a treaty would leave them open to royal retribution, and they naturally favoured a new offensive war, led by Essex. The peace party won the argument, but their rivals helped to influence the terms.

Thus, on 1 February 1643, the earl of Northumberland led the delegation to Oxford with a new set of peace proposals. Parliament's demands were similar to those made in the Nineteen Propositions eight months earlier. Appointments to church and state offices would have to be made in consultation with Parliament, and Parliament would also have a degree of control over the armed forces. Key royalists would have to be surrendered for trial, and the king was invited to return to London. At this stage of the war, such terms were unlikely to be taken seriously at Oxford. Some of the king's advisers, such as the earls of Dorset and Bath, were willing to make concessions to bring the war to an end; but the 'ultra-royalists', notably Rupert, Lord Digby, and the circle around the queen, urged the king to renew the war

ROBERT DEVEREUX EARLE OF ESSEX &EWE VISCOUNT HERREFORD LORD FERRYES of Charley Boucheyer & Loveyne, his excellency & Generall of the Forces rayfed by the authority of the Parliament for the defence of the Protestant Religion, King & Kingdome &     4th October 1643

**Figure 3**   Robert Devereux, 3rd Earl of Essex depicted as Captain General on horseback. Engraving by Wenceslaus Hollar.

and dictate terms when the 'rebels' had been defeated. The king agreed with the latter view, but he was content to allow peace talks to drift along into April, while preparing his troops for a new campaign.

## 'KING PYM'

John Pym (born 1584) was the scion of a well-established Somerset family, and a trained lawyer, but his reputation was made during the 1620s when, as MP for Tavistock in Devon, he became a prominent opponent of the religious and political policies of Charles I. His activities won him the respect of leading puritans, including the earls of Bedford and Warwick and Viscount Saye, and he was close to godly members of the gentry across England, including Sir Thomas Barrington and Oliver St John. Such connections made Pym an influential opposition figure in the early months of the Long Parliament, and he was nicknamed 'King Pym' for his eagerness to secure wide executive powers for committees that he chaired. From the summer of 1642, he was the leading light of the 'war party' in the Commons. Pym died in December 1643, just after the alliance with the Scots – which he had masterminded – had been sealed.

The failure of the 'Oxford Peace' left the war parties in both Oxford and Westminster in control of policy. Rupert and his allies encouraged the king to extend his territories, and during the spring and early summer the royalists gained a series of notable successes. Hopton was at last able to break out of Cornwall, having defeated the parliamentarians at Stratton in May, and he joined other forces in taking most of Devon and Somerset in the next few weeks. Newcastle pushed south, defeating the Fairfaxes at Adwalton Moor in June. The Oxford army reinforced its position in Berkshire and Oxfordshire, and put pressure on parliamentarian Buckinghamshire.

In response, Essex was sluggish. His army had not marched from Windsor until the Oxford treaty was definitely dead, and, although he had taken Reading, he did not make any real progress against Oxford, and his troops received a nasty reverse at Chalgrove, where the celebrated 'patriot' John Hampden was killed.

Parliament's local forces were also hard-pressed in the east and west midlands, and the most successful of the subordinate commanders, Sir William Waller, was forced to abandon his gains in the Severn Valley to counter Hopton in Somerset. He received a bloody nose at Lansdown, outside Bath, on 5 July, and his army was obliterated at Roundway Down, in Wiltshire, barely a week later. On 26 July, Bristol fell to Rupert, and most of Dorset soon followed, leaving Parliament with only a handful of ports strung along the south coast: Plymouth, Exeter, Lyme Regis, and Poole. In early August, the king moved his main army against the parliamentarian city of Gloucester.

The 'month of victories' for the king shocked Parliament. Essex, under attack for his lack of success, was forced to give semi-autonomous commands to Waller in the south and the earl of Manchester in the 'Eastern Association' centred on East Anglia. Essex was also forced into action to relieve Gloucester, which he did with surprising speed, only to be cut off by the king, whose army blocked the London Road at Newbury. The battle that ensued on 20 September was long and hard-fought and indecisive; but it did force the king to withdraw north, allowing Essex to reach London, where he was greeted as a hero.

There was little disguising the seriousness of the situation, however. On 15 September, five days before Newbury, the king's representatives had signed a truce, known as the 'cessation', with the Irish Catholic rebels, which would release Protestant troops to support the king in England. Reports of the progress of these

## CESSATION AND COVENANT, SEPTEMBER 1643

Since February 1643, the king had been in talks with the Irish Catholic rebels, now organized into the 'Confederation of Kilkenny'. His aim was to arrange a truce that would allow the large Protestant army, commanded by the marquess of Ormond, to be transported across the Irish Sea to reinforce the royalist forces in England and Wales. This 'cessation of arms' was signed on 15 September, and in the next few months Irish regiments arrived in the north-west and south-west of England. Their contribution to the war was not decisive, however, and Ormond and other commanders in Ireland distrusted the Irish Catholics, and were reluctant to part with their best men. The truce eventually collapsed in the autumn of 1646.

Also in 1643, Parliament was talking to the Scots. The Scots had originally remained aloof from the war in England, although there was no secret which side they favoured. In August, it was finally decided to sign a binding treaty, known as the Solemn League and Covenant. This was in the form of a religious oath, to preserve the Scottish church and reform the English one along Presbyterian lines, to defeat the enemies of both nations, while promising to 'preserve and defend the king's majesty's person and authority'. The Covenant was signed by the parliamentarians on 25 September, and a large army of Scottish 'covenanters' crossed the Tweed in January 1644. The military alliance would prove a disappointment for Parliament, however, and the religious terms – crucial to the Scots – were not always honoured by English politicians seeking to make peace with the king on their own terms.

negotiations, and the successes of the royalists in England during the summer, had encouraged Parliament to conclude their own long-running discussions with the Scots. The Solemn League and Covenant was signed by MPs and peers on 25 September. The new campaigning season would see the involvement of large contingents of foreign troops on English soil for the first time during the war.

# War in the balance, 1644–5

The new year of 1644 saw increasing political tensions in both Westminster and Oxford. The cessation with the Irish Confederates had raised fears among some royalists that the king intended to make a permanent peace with the Catholic rebels, and to ship thousands of their troops to England. The king called a rival Parliament at Oxford in January to raise further money for the war and to bolster his authority, but only about a third of the members attended, and very few defected from Westminster. The recent victories had resulted in open rivalry between the pro-war 'Cavaliers', and especially between Rupert and Lord Digby, leading one courtier to complain that 'we have such a seminary of faction both in the court and the army, as God must work miracles if the king would be well served'.

Parliament was facing problems of its own. The death of John Pym in December had left a power vacuum, while the advent of the Scots (whose army of 21,000 crossed the Tweed in January) had alienated the earl of Essex, who felt his military supremacy was under threat. In the absence of Pym, the task of conciliating Essex fell to another senior MP, the godly lawyer Oliver St John, but he had only limited success, and as 1644 continued the earl made common cause with Holles and the peace party. They were opposed by the Saye–St John faction, which now had the removal of Essex high on its agenda. Their Scottish allies pushed for the joint management of the war, and this resulted in the creation of a new executive committee, the Committee of Both Kingdoms, in February. This included peers and MPs of both sides as well as a number of Scots, but it was far from being an attempt to bury differences. Saye, St John, the younger Sir Henry Vane, and their supporters – now including the earl of Northumberland – dominated the new committee, and its powers, which included the overall management of the war effort, effectively trumped the authority of Essex as lord general.

The political crises in both camps did not help the new campaigning season, which began early in the new year of 1644. There were disappointments for either side. The arrival of five veteran regiments from Ireland at Chester had initially forced the parliamentarians to retreat to Nantwich in January, but a sudden attack by Sir Thomas Fairfax defeated the royalists outside the town, and many of the Irish Protestant troops promptly changed sides. In the north, the Scots soon overran Northumberland and Durham, but then became bogged down in a long drawn-out siege of Newcastle.

In the spring, Rupert relieved Newark in Nottingham-shire in an exhilarating lightning strike, but then retreated to the Welsh borders to recruit more men. And in the south the victory of Waller over Hopton at Cheriton, near Winchester, was not followed by a decisive advance by the man lauded in the press as 'William the Conqueror'. Essex remained inactive in the home counties, while the king became even more defensive, withdrawing his army to Oxford after Cheriton. The success of the Fairfaxes in Yorkshire had a similar effect on the marquess of Newcastle, who pulled his men back to York, which was then besieged by an Anglo-Scottish force. For a time, it looked like the civil war would degenerate – as had recent wars on the continent – into a series of prolonged sieges.

Characteristically, it was the dashing Prince Rupert who cut the Gordian Knot. In the late spring, he went on the offensive, marching into the north-west, where he relieved the earl of Derby's house at Lathom, sacked Bolton, and took Liverpool. The king, who still feared that he would be trapped in Oxford, was in two minds whether Rupert's next move should be to reinforce Oxford or to relieve York. In an unhelpfully ambiguous letter, he suggested the latter was the priority, and that a pitched battle with the parliamentarians was desirable.

Following a circuitous route, Rupert's men entered York from the east on 1 July, and forced the besiegers to abandon their lines and withdraw to the south-west. The next day, he provoked a battle on Marston Moor, and was decisively beaten by the Anglo-Scottish army. Rupert escaped to fight another day, but there was no hiding the fact that the crushing defeat had effectively lost the north for Charles I. York soon surrendered, and the earl of Newcastle went into exile with the parting words: 'I will not endure the laughter of the court'.

Yet Parliament's great victory did not bring an end to the war. In part, this was because the victorious generals were divided as to the next move, as the earl of Manchester was concerned that 'total victory' might give the whip-hand to the Saye–St John faction in the Committee of Both Kingdoms, and the Scottish earl of Leven was keen to continue the siege of Newcastle. Furthermore, news came of the defeat of Waller by the king at Cropredy Bridge, and of the decision by the earl of Essex, ignoring the advice of the committee, to march into the south-west to relieve Lyme and take Exeter.

Essex's campaign started promisingly enough, but by mid-July all was not well. The king, with Hopton, was hard on Essex's heels, and by August the earl made the crazy decision to advance into Cornwall, rather than seek shelter in Plymouth. More royalists gathered, and soon Essex was trapped at Lostwithiel. On 31 August, his cavalry managed to break out, but on 2 September his infantry was forced to surrender. Essex escaped in a small boat from Fowey. He was lord general in name alone.

Just as the parliamentarians had not followed up their success at Marston Moor, so the king failed to capitalize on his victory at Lostwithiel. A desultory siege of Plymouth ensued, and the main royalist army did not march eastwards until mid-October. Rupert remained in Bristol, licking his wounds, throughout September and October.

Both sides were beset by doubts during the autumn of 1644, fuelled by factional divisions among the politicians and personal rivalries between individual commanders. This was all too apparent among the parliamentarians during the second battle of Newbury on 27 October. The king's army had been brought to battle by a superior parliamentarian force made up of the men of Manchester and Waller and the remnants of Essex's army, but they failed to work together, and the attack was confused and indecisive, allowing the royalists to withdraw to Oxford, relieving Donnington Castle en route.

The fiasco led to the famous exchange between Manchester and his lieutenant-general, Oliver Cromwell. Cromwell told the Commons that Manchester had refused to renew the attack on the king, with the defeatist sentiment that 'if we beat the king 99 times he would be king still, and his posterity, and we subjects still; but if he beat us but once we should be hanged, and our posterity undone'. Manchester retorted that Cromwell was a troublemaker; 'his expressions were sometimes against the nobility, that he hoped to live to see never a noble in England', and he had showed 'contempt' for the Presbyterian church and 'animosity' against the Scots. There is no evidence that Cromwell was a social revolutionary, but his religious views, and his opposition to the Scots, were already well known. His real crime was his close association with the Saye–St John faction, which was already plotting the removal of both Manchester and Essex as generals, and the creation of a new army that would win the war without Scottish help.

This desire to put the war on a more 'professional' footing was also apparent in Oxford, and in November 1644 the king made Rupert his captain-general, with overall command of the army. Yet Charles gave with one hand and took away with the other, for he was soon persuaded (probably by Rupert's rival, Lord Digby) to give command of a semi-autonomous force, based in the west country, to the new general of horse, Lord Goring. This division of the army, and the suspicions that were growing between Rupert and key figures at Oxford, would do much to ruin the king's cause over the next six months. In the winter of 1644–5, however, it appeared far more likely that Parliament would tear itself apart first.

## GEORGE LORD DIGBY

Digby (born 1612) was the eldest son of the 1st earl of Bristol. He was born and brought up in Spain, where his father was James I's ambassador, and educated at Oxford. A handsome and charming man, Digby would have risen high in the royal court but for the tensions between his father and Charles I, and his own marriage to the daughter of an opposition peer, the earl of Bedford. An opponent of the crown in the early stages of the Long Parliament, Digby suddenly changed sides in April 1641, denouncing the trial of the king's adviser, the earl of Strafford. This earned him a peerage from the king and the hatred of his former colleagues in the Commons. Digby joined the king in 1642 and was made secretary of state in 1643. From this position of influence, he used his courtly skills to persuade the king to undertake risky policies, and to turn his back not only on those royalists who called for peace, but also on his most capable general, Prince Rupert.

The recriminations that followed the parliamentarian failure at Newbury polarized opinion at Westminster, as the Saye–St John group solidified into what would become known as the 'Independent' interest, opposed by the Essex–Holles or 'Presbyterian' faction. The names were derived from religious positions, but only a few on either side could be described as Congregationalists or rigid Presbyterians. Instead, the factions were separated by their positions on the war and on the role of the Scots. For the Independents, only total victory would do; and, when Parliament dictated its terms to the king, there was to be no interference from Scotland. The Presbyterians favoured a negotiated peace, and saw the Scots as important parties in any settlement, not least because they were needed to suppress the Irish rebellion – which was seen by all sides as an urgent priority after the civil war ended.

The row between Manchester and Cromwell, and the plotting against Essex, was but the preliminary sparring before a full-scale struggle for control of the war effort and, with it, the type of peace that would follow. The next round began in December, when Cromwell called for the professionalization of the army and the resignation of the amateur soldiers – specifically the MPs and peers – who now enjoyed most of the senior commands. This motion was backed by Vane and other Independents, and led to the so-called 'Self-Denying Ordinance', passed on 19 December. The majority required to pass this ordinance depended on its being sold as a non-partisan measure, with Independents such as Cromwell losing their military positions alongside Essex, Manchester, and Waller. There is little doubt, however, that this was part of a longstanding plan to remove Essex, in particular, and his supporters recognized this on 17 December, when they narrowly failed to have the earl exempted from the new ordinance.

Hot on the heels of the Self-Denying Ordinance came a move to reorganize Parliament's forces into a single new army – the New Model Army. Again, this had been part of the Independent programme for several months, although it was framed as an impartial attempt to solve the very real problem of a divided command. The new general was Sir Thomas Fairfax, a young and successful commander from the north, who was connected – but not too closely – with key members of the Independent party, including the earl of Northumberland. Fairfax's appointment was agreed by a vote of 21 January 1645, with Vane and Cromwell telling in favour, and the leading Presbyterians, Holles and Stapilton, acting as tellers against. The Presbyterian-dominated House of Lords did its best to delay ratifying Fairfax's commission, and refused to accept his choice of officers (which included no Scots at all) until early April. The New Model Army, with Fairfax at its head, was still presented as Parliament's army; but the critic who described it as 'Fairfax his Independent army' was not far off the mark.

## Parliament's victory, 1645–6

In the early weeks of 1645, as the wrangles over the Self-Denying Ordinance and the New Model Army continued at Westminster, moderates on both sides sought to reopen peace talks. The Uxbridge discussions were the initiative of the Scots and their Presbyterian allies, and the terms offered to the king were correspondingly inflexible. The king was to take the Covenant, abolish

## SIR EDWARD HYDE

Hyde was born into a Wiltshire gentry family in 1609. He was educated at Oxford and the Middle Temple, and became a prosperous lawyer and friend of the intellectual set known as the 'Great Tew Circle' in the 1630s. He was elected as MP for the Cornish seat of Saltash in 1640, and was at first a critic of the crown; but the attack on the church, and in particular the attempt to abolish bishops, encouraged him to join the king by 1642. Thereafter, he became a privy councillor and chancellor of the exchequer, and was among the king's most important advisers during the first civil war – although his advice was not always heeded. Hyde opposed the policy of pursuing total victory – as advocated by Rupert and Digby – and he was a key figure in the peace treaties at Oxford in 1643 and Uxbridge in 1645. The failure of the latter left Hyde out of favour with Charles I, although he continued to be loyal to the Stuarts, and at the Restoration was made earl of Clarendon.

bishops and the English church hierarchy, and introduce a Presbyterian system instead. The army and navy were to be under the control of Parliament and the Scots on a permanent basis, and the Irish war prosecuted vigorously. Unsurprisingly, Charles baulked at such demands, and the talks broke down – to the dismay of not only the Presbyterians, but also those royalists, led by Sir Edward Hyde and the marquess of Hertford, who were desperate for peace. The failure of the Uxbridge treaty discredited the doves on both sides, and for the next year the hawks were in the ascendant.

Despite the delays caused by the Lords' opposition to the details of the New Model Army ordinance, Fairfax was able to recruit his new army ready for the campaigning season, and he took to the field in April. The army was not yet complete, however, and Fairfax remained at the beck and call of Parliament's executive, the Committee of Both Kingdoms, which had retained its overall control of military affairs. It was at the committee's behest that Fairfax led his men west, in an attempt to relieve

Taunton in Somerset, besieged by Lord Goring. Before he had accomplished this, the committee called him back to Oxford, which they hoped might be gained through a treacherous plot by its governor. This proved a canard, but Fairfax's approach to the royalist capital, and the success of Cromwell (working out his period of notice as Manchester's lieutenant-general) in the region in April and May, caused the king to muster as many men as he could at Stow-on-the-Wold.

Once again, royalist counsels were hopelessly divided, with Rupert favouring a northern campaign, while other advisers called for a westward attack on Fairfax's advancing troops. The result was another uneasy compromise, with Goring returning to the siege of Taunton, and Rupert attempting to draw the New Model Army away from Oxford northwards. The diversionary tactic worked, and Fairfax followed Rupert into the east midlands in the hope of bringing him to battle – a task made all the more urgent by the royalist sack of Leicester on 30 May, which caused great alarm at Westminster. In a rare flash of inspiration, the Committee of Both Kingdoms released its control over Fairfax, and issued him with broad instructions to engage the enemy as best he could. This gave him the independence he needed, and in early June he moved gradually closer to the royalists in Northamptonshire, gathering in supplies and new recruits. There he was joined by Cromwell, who had recently been appointed as lieutenant-general of the New Model Army, even though this contravened the terms of the Self-Denying Ordinance.

Rupert was aware of the approaching enemy, but, thanks to the inadequacy of his scouts, he did not realize how close they were until it was almost too late. Nor did he know just how large a force was confronting him. The royalists were still waiting for reinforcements, especially from Goring, who ignored repeated requests to send his cavalry across from Somerset. Rupert favoured a withdrawal, but others around the king, notably Digby, persuaded the king that victory over the raw troops of the 'New Noddle' would be a mere trifle. As a result, the king's army was annihilated at Naseby on 14 June.

The political fall-out from Naseby was dramatic. Fairfax and Cromwell shared the honours, and were hailed in the press as heroes, to the delight of their friends in the Independent party. The capture of the royal correspondence, known as the 'king's cabinet', revealed the extent of Charles's scheme to bring Irish Catholic troops to England. The supporters of peace fell silent, and, when Rupert, who had returned to Bristol, urged the king to negotiate with Parliament, he received a terse reply from Charles: 'speaking as a mere soldier or statesman, I must say that there is no probability but of my ruin; yet as a Christian, I must tell you that God will not suffer rebels or traitors to prosper'. Such an attitude would prolong the war for another year, and eventually lead to the royal martyrdom in January 1649.

From June 1645, the New Model Army went from one victory to another. Fairfax lost no time in marching into the south-west, reaching Dorchester on 3 July, and forcing Goring to abandon the siege of Taunton. At Langport on 10 July, Fairfax assaulted a strongly defended position and routed Goring's army. Over the next few weeks, Bridgwater, Bath, and Sherborne Castle all fell to the New Model Army, and on 23 August Fairfax lay siege to Bristol. The storming of the city, on 10 September, was bloody, and Rupert was lucky to be able to halt the onslaught and sue for peace. The agreement he made with Fairfax was the best Rupert could hope for in a desperate position, but the king was furious, stripping the prince of his command and ordering him to leave the country forthwith. Charles was eventually persuaded to come to a reconciliation of sorts with his nephew, but Rupert played no further part in the war.

Lord Digby now became the king's chief adviser, encouraging Charles to make renewed efforts to make a deal with the Catholic Irish. It was a forlorn hope. During the autumn, Fairfax continued his relentless advance into the south-west, entering Devon in October, defeating a ragged force under Hopton at Torrington in February 1646, before entering Cornwall a few days later. In the meantime, Cromwell was dealing with pockets of resistance in Hampshire and Wiltshire, taking Winchester and sacking the great Catholic fortress of Basing House in October. By the end of April, the army had reunited to besiege Oxford itself, which surrendered on terms in June.

The war was over, but there was no sign of a lasting settlement, as factional conflict intensified. This was partly the fault of the king, who had refused to negotiate even in defeat, and instead slipped out of Oxford and took refuge with the Scottish forces around Newark. This appears to have been the master plan of Lord Digby. Having failed to secure aid from the Irish, Digby and his allies had been in talks with the Scots for several months, in the hope that they would support the king in the face of unacceptable demands from the Independents at Westminster. In some ways, this was a shrewd move that would divide the rival parliamentarian factions still further, as the Presbyterians naturally sided with their Scottish allies – not least because they possessed the only army capable of squaring up to the New Model Army if the need arose. Involving the Scots was also extremely divisive among the royalists, with Hyde, Hertford, and others being so bitterly opposed to a settlement dictated by the Scottish covenanters that they contemplated approaching the Independents as the lesser of two evils.

Whether or not Charles's gamble paid off, it could only increase the parliamentarians' distrust of the king and his advisers. Nearly four years of civil war, with all the death and destruction that they had entailed, and total defeat of the royalists in the field, had not been enough to persuade the king that he might be mistaken.

# 3

# The search for settlement, 1646–9

## Factional politics, 1646–7

The end of the first civil war also saw the end of any pretence of unity on either side of the political divide. The king's flight to the Scottish army appalled many royalists, who saw the Scots as the original rebels, whose actions in the later 1630s had triggered civil war and defeat in England. Sir Edward Hyde declared that he 'thought it an unkingly thing…to ask relief of those who had done all the mischief'. While the royalist hawks, especially Lord Digby, encouraged the king to continue to seek allies outside England – whether in Scotland, Ireland, or France – Hyde and his friends sought to make peace in England, and hoped to strengthen what was a very weak bargaining position by playing the parliamentarian factions off against each other. For his part, Charles was happy to entertain both plans, while pursuing his usual tactic of intransigence. When offered peace terms, known as the Newcastle Propositions, by the Scots and their Presbyterian allies in July 1646, the king refused, unwilling in particular to agree to the religious clauses that would abolish the Anglican Church.

The king's refusal of the Newcastle Propositions had an immediate effect on the factions at Westminster, dashing any hopes among the Presbyterians that they might be able to outmanoeuvre

## THE NEWCASTLE PROPOSITIONS, JULY 1646

The terms of the new proposals were based on those presented at Uxbridge in 1645, but with harsher measures that reflected Parliament's victory over the king in the field. The main heads were:

- Parliament would in future choose all officers of state.
- Parliament would control the armed forces for twenty years.
- The king would accept the Covenant, abolish bishops, and implement Presbyterian forms.
- A long list of active royalists would be barred from office, and fifty-eight named individuals excepted from pardon, and thus open to treason charges.

their Independent rivals, who claimed the victories of the New Model Army as their own. Worse was to come. In August, the Scots, disillusioned by the king's awkwardness, agreed to withdraw their army from England and to hand over Charles to Parliament's custody, in return for money to cover its arrears of pay; and in September the Presbyterian leader, the earl of Essex, died after a stroke. These developments were a blow to those royalists hoping for Scottish support for the king, and the failure of the king's lord lieutenant of Ireland, the marquess of Ormond, to agree a lasting peace treaty with the Confederate Catholics meant there was no chance of assistance from that quarter. As a result, in the late autumn of 1646, there seemed to be only one likely outcome: that Hyde and his allies would arrange a settlement with the dominant Independent party at Westminster.

The withdrawal of the Scottish army from English soil in January 1647, and the surrender of the king to Parliament's custody, was seen by many in England and Scotland as the ultimate betrayal. As the earl of Lauderdale warned, giving up the king 'would make them to be hissed at by all nations; yea, the dogs in the street would piss upon them'. In the longer term, this dishonourable episode made some Scots question their most fundamental beliefs, including the Solemn League and Covenant, and helped the king's friends north of the border to raise support for future interventions in English politics.

At Westminster, the Independents were triumphant, but in fact the departure of the Scots was one reason for the resurgence of the Presbyterian faction in the spring of 1647. With their unpopular allies removed, the Presbyterians would enjoy wider support in England; and there was no longer any justification for retaining the New Model Army, which was already proving a strain on the country's finances. Furthermore, the 'recruiter' elections, to replace those royalist MPs removed from the Commons, had given the Presbyterians a clear majority in the lower House. The result, in March 1647, was a vote by the Commons to disband the New Model Army, and ship part of it to Ireland to reinforce the Protestant forces there.

In principle, the reconquest of Ireland was the obvious next campaign for the veterans of the New Model Army, and many officers, including Cromwell, were not against such a move. The Presbyterians, however, played their hand very badly. Instead of heeding the soldiers' demands for the payment of the arrears and for legal indemnity against prosecution for their past actions, the Commons sent commissioners to the army headquarters at Saffron Walden in Essex to demand an immediate decision as to which regiments should go to Ireland. The predictably angry response led to a massive overreaction at Westminster, where Denzil Holles drafted a motion warning that troublemakers would be 'looked upon and proceeded against as enemies of the state and disturbers of the public peace'. In April, there was a further confrontation, when the Presbyterian choice of non-New Model Army commanders for the Irish campaign was met with shouts of 'Fairfax and Cromwell, and we all go!'

As the stand-off continued, the regiments began to organize politically, electing 'agitators' to represent ordinary soldiers as well as officers, and in early June a junior officer – apparently with the knowledge of his superiors – took a force to the king's lodgings at Holdenby House in Northamptonshire, and removed Charles to Newmarket in Suffolk, where he became the 'guest' of the New Model Army. By the middle of the same month, the army had issued impeachment proceedings against the '11 members' – the leading Presbyterians at Westminster, including Holles. Finally, on 25 June, the army moved closer to London, in an attempt to bring direct pressure to bear on Parliament. Fearing a military coup, the 11 members withdrew from the Commons, and the army in turn retreated to Reading, installing the king at the nearby mansion of Caversham Park.

In the next few weeks, the army and its Independent allies began their own negotiations with Charles. Cromwell's son-in-law, Henry Ireton, produced new peace propositions, the *Heads of the Proposals*, which constituted the most lenient terms the king would ever be offered. A new council would advise the king; Parliament would control the army for ten years; and the Anglican Church would be revived, but as one of many different Christian beliefs and forms of worship, all enjoying 'liberty of conscience'. These were precisely the terms that Hyde and other moderate royalists were looking for; but the king prevaricated, in the hope that the parliamentarian factions would soon destroy each other. This was a reasonable gamble in the circumstances.

When the *Heads of the Proposals* were debated at Westminster on 20 July, there were riots, and the London mob, encouraged by the 11 members and their friends, invaded the Houses of Parliament, forcing the Independent MPs to take refuge with the army. The so-called 'forcing of the Houses' began on 26 July and lasted just over a week. During this period, there was a real risk of a new civil war, as the London militia regiments mustered to defend the capital. As one royalist reported, 'the Presbyterian party do think they can near match the army with foot if they will fight', even if they acknowledged that their cavalry was inferior. Undaunted, the New Model Army advanced to Hounslow Heath on 3 August, and to Southwark on the 4th, before entering London the next day. Military opposition crumbled at their approach, and their political opponents fled. With the New Model Army came the Speakers of the two Houses, fourteen peers and around a hundred MPs. It was this Independent caucus that would dominate proceedings in Parliament for much of the next year.

# The rise of army radicalism, 1647

From the summer of 1647, the position of the New Model Army changed. Instead of being in effect the military wing of the Independent party, the army came to dominate its old political masters. The politicization of the New Model Army first began in the spring, when the regiments were forced to organize themselves in opposition to pressure from the Presbyterian-dominated Parliament. In later months, the army not only proposed its own peace terms but also intervened directly at Westminster, forcing out the Presbyterians and ensuring the hegemony of the Independents. In the weeks that followed, senior officers such as Fairfax, Cromwell, and Ireton played a crucial role in pushing through measures to rescind legislation passed during the 'forcing of the Houses' in late July and early August. They also had the difficult job of keeping the more radical elements of the rank and file and junior officers, frustrated by the slow rate of reform,

## THE LEVELLERS

The Levellers were a loose coalition of London radicals, including John Lilburne, John Wildman, and William Walwyn, which feared that the king would be allowed back unconditionally or on very lenient terms in 1647. They were notorious for their championing of far-reaching reforms in government and society, including the redistribution (or 'levelling') of wealth and power. It was for this reason that their nickname was coined, allegedly by Charles I, who called it 'a most apt title for such a despicable and desperate knot

to be known by, that endeavour to cast down and level the enclosures of nobility, gentry and propriety, to make us all even; so that
every Jack shall be a gentleman, and every gentleman be made a
Jack'. The links between the Levellers and the radicals in the army
gradually grew stronger, as seen in the events that led to the trial
of the king, and the army mutiny in 1649.

from open mutiny. Discontent was fomented by a new, and very
alarming, political grouping known as the Levellers, who were
opposed to any settlement with the king.

The clash between the senior officers and the radicals came at
the army headquarters, now established at Putney to the west of
London, in late October and early November. A general council
of the army, called to discuss the *Heads of the Proposals*, found
itself debating instead a new pamphlet, *The Case of the Army Truly
Stated*, which argued against a negotiated peace with the king,
claiming that power rested with the people. This was seconded by
a 'Leveller' manifesto, *The Agreement of the People*, which presented
a completely new system of government.

In the face of this radical agenda, Cromwell and Ireton tried
to manage the 'Putney Debates' as best they could, working to
prevent an irrevocable split within the army. Especially worry-
ing were repeated calls for the king to be put on trial as 'that
man of blood', who had waged war against his own people. The
senior officers could only maintain unity by dissolving the general
council without a conclusion. The continuing distrust between
commanders and their men can also be seen in November, when a
general rendezvous of New Model Army regiments was changed
to three meetings in three different locations, to ensure that no
general mutiny would be possible. The first of these musters,
held at Ware in Hertfordshire, threatened to turn ugly, as soldiers
turned up wearing copies of the *Agreement* in their hats, with the
scrawled slogan 'England's freedoms, soldiers' rights'. Only a show
of authority by Fairfax and his officers, who rode through the

## OLIVER CROMWELL AND HENRY IRETON

The relationship between the New Model Army's lieutenant-general, Oliver Cromwell, and its commissary-general, Henry Ireton, was complex. Ireton became Cromwell's son-in-law in 1646, and the two men found common ground in their religious beliefs, and in their shared military service. Their approach to politics was very different – Ireton was a radical intellectual, Cromwell more pragmatic and impulsive – but they clearly sparked off each other. In the late 1640s, while Cromwell mixed vigorous action and charismatic leadership with periods of doubt and uncertainty, Ireton pursued a remorseless political programme, revealed in the *Heads of the Proposals*, the *Remonstrance of the Army*, and the abortive attempts to produce a written constitution in the winter of 1648–9. It is arguable that without the qualities of both men the 'English Revolution' would have been very different – if it had happened at all.

ranks confiscating the pamphlets, and the subsequent arrest of the ringleaders, prevented the situation from getting out of hand.

In the longer term, the quietening of the mutinous spirits within the army was the result of political developments. In November, the king escaped from his new lodgings at Hampton Court and, after a half-hearted attempt to take ship for the continent, eventually arrived at Carisbrooke Castle on the Isle of Wight, where he was again put under house arrest. This escapade provoked the army leadership to toughen its line towards the king, much to the delight of the radicals. Cromwell, in particular, appears to have turned against Charles from this time onwards. The royal agent, Sir John Berkeley, who had negotiated with the generals at Reading the previous summer, now found all avenues barred. On 28 November, he tried to secure a hearing, but Cromwell, Ireton, and other contacts now 'saluted me coldly, and had their countenance very changed towards me'.

Other doors were also closing. The House of Lords tried to pursue another peace settlement, called the *Four Bills*, in a last attempt to break the deadlock, but Charles rejected them out of hand. The king's attitude shows that he calculated that the new approach from Parliament would be best used as a bargaining counter in another set of negotiations – with the Scots. By the autumn of 1647, the Scots were at last prepared to atone for their previous act in abandoning the king, and, more importantly, to prevent a peace dictated by the New Model Army and the radical Independents, that would abandon the Presbyterian church settlement agreed in the Solemn League and Covenant.

On 26 December, Charles agreed the Engagement with the Scots, securing Scottish military intervention in return for settling Presbyterian church government for three years. The taking of the Solemn League and Covenant was no longer part of the package. The moderated tone of the agreement reflects the new influence of Charles's cousin, the duke of Hamilton, over the Scottish government; it was also a success for the pro-Scots royalist lobby, headed by Henry Jermyn and Sir John Culpepper. The Engagement was a plan cooked up by groups with only very modest followings in their own camps. Hamilton faced vigorous opposition from the hard-line covenanters in Scotland, while Hyde dismissed the new agreement as 'most scandalous and derogatory to the honour and interest of the English nation'. Worse still, the Engagement with the Scots was an open secret, and in January 1648 an angry Westminster Parliament passed a 'vote of no addresses', which ended all further peace talks with their perfidious king.

# The second civil war and its aftermath, 1648

During the spring of 1648, it became increasingly clear that the Scots were not the only ones prepared to give Charles I a second chance. The growing influence of the New Model Army, and the refusal of the Independent-dominated Parliament to continue peace talks, led to a surge of popular support for the king, or rather for his office, which was seen as safeguarding the rule of law. There had been riots in December in favour of the traditional Christmas holiday – banned in 1644 by parliamentary ordinance – and unrest continued in the next few months, with many counties in southern England sending petitions calling for a peace treaty with the king.

There was also growing resentment in Ireland, not least in the southern province of Munster, where the lord president, Lord Inchiquin, found himself starved of money and supplies by his Independent enemies. Inchiquin suddenly defected to the king in April. In the same month, royalists seized the vital border towns of Carlisle and Berwick, preparatory to a Scottish invasion of England. Unrest in South Wales also brought an open revolt, led by former parliamentarians such as Roland Laugharne, and, although the New Model Army defeated the rebels at St Fagans in May, Pembroke Castle held out for the king. Trouble had also broken out in Kent, Surrey, and Essex. Worryingly, these counties had been staunchly parliamentarian during the first civil war. More obviously royalist areas, such as the south-west and north-west, also saw uprisings, although most of these were swiftly dealt with by local forces.

The second civil war, as it is usually known, was in reality a series of uncoordinated rebellions and risings, with little chance of success. The motley alliance of royalists, Presbyterians, Irish, and Scots was beset with jealousy and mistrust. As one northern royalist put it, 'although they hated the Scots as bad as the Turks, yet they would all join either with Scot or Turk to suppress the Independents and restore the king'. Nor was it clear what sort of a settlement a Scottish 'restoration' would entail.

The crucial factor that led to the failure of the uprising was the delay of the Scottish army in crossing the border. The prospect of a new war in England, on behalf of Charles I, was as divisive in Scotland as it was in England, and there was no love lost between the radical supporters of the Covenant, led by the marquess of Argyll, and the Engagers under Hamilton. Argyll refused to cooperate, and he and his supporters did their best to hamper the raising of a new army. Only in July had the Scottish force reached the border, and Hamilton's slow march through north-west England was brought to a sudden halt at Preston in Lancashire, when the Scots were attacked by Cromwell on 17 August, and completely routed. In the meantime, Fairfax had bottled up the main force of English royalists in the Essex town of Colchester, which was subjected to a close siege. Colchester surrendered on 28 August, and the royalist rising came to an abrupt end.

The Scottish defeat had led to a coup in Edinburgh, with Argyll and the anti-Engagers seizing power in what became known as the 'Whiggamore Raid'. Hamilton and his supporters were excluded from office, and the remains of their army disbanded. Cromwell marched into Scotland after Preston to ensure that Argyll's plans were enforced, and then returned to Yorkshire to oversee the siege of the last royalist stronghold, Pontefract. Ormond, who had returned to Ireland during the summer, began new talks with the Catholic Irish in September, but they were too late to influence the outcome of the war.

An early result of the second civil war was the fragmentation of the factions at Westminster. The Presbyterians were divided by the question of whether or not to join the rebellion. The Independents also split, into a radical wing that supported the army, and a more moderate group, which joined the remaining Presbyterians in the Commons to call for new talks with the king. This new enthusiasm for negotiation was apparent as early as the end of April, when there were calls in the Commons for the ban on peace talks to be lifted, and in July some MPs even backed an unconditional treaty with the king, without firm religious and political restrictions on his authority.

Formal negotiations, at Newport on the Isle of Wight, opened on 18 September. For the next few weeks, terms were discussed,

but the old stumbling block remained. Despite his earlier promises to the Scots, in his talks with Parliament the king made it clear
he would not accept the abolition of bishops or the establishment
of a Presbyterian system of church government, even temporar-
ily. The army greeted this new initiative with dismay, fearing that
Parliament would allow the king soft terms, and thus surrender
everything that they had fought for since 1642. Their response
was the *Remonstrance of the Army*, drafted by Ireton (perhaps with
assistance from the Leveller John Lilburne) and agreed by the
council of officers on 18 November. This manifesto promised a
new constitution, similar to that proposed by *The Agreement of
the People*, and based on the principle that the king's power was
delegated from the people's representatives in Parliament. The
*Remonstrance* also called for the purging of Parliament and the
trial of the king, who was seen as personally responsible for the
bloodshed of the renewed civil war. He was, it stated, 'guilty of
the highest treason against the law' and 'of all the innocent blood
spilt'. The king was also deemed guilty of defying the will of God,
so clearly expressed in the New Model Army's victories in 1645
and 1646. He was, as Cromwell wrote on 25 November, 'this
man, against whom the Lord hath witnessed'.

Parliament rejected the army's document out of hand, insisting instead on pursuing the Newport talks with the king, voting
on 5 December that the Newport terms would be the basis for
a new treaty. It was this that triggered yet another intervention
at Westminster by the New Model Army, on 6 December, when
Colonel Thomas Pride and other senior officers stationed troops
at the doors of the Commons chamber, refusing entry to those
opposed to the army, and imprisoning their most dangerous
enemies. Of 471 eligible to sit in the Commons, only around
200 remained. 'Pride's Purge' had the support of both Fairfax
and Cromwell, although neither man was present – and Cromwell was careful to delay his arrival in London on the evening
of the 6th, to make sure he could not be blamed for the army's
actions. Troops occupied London on 8 December, and forced

the city authorities to pay for their upkeep. The army coup had succeeded. But what was to happen to the king?

## The regicide

The trial and execution of Charles I was not an inevitable result of the civil wars. The outbreak of war in 1642 had been a rebellion against an oppressive and inflexible king, not an attempted revolution. And, as we have seen, it was only the involvement of the army in politics from the summer of 1647, and in particular the bloodshed of the second civil war, that raised the possibility of bringing the king to trial for his crimes against the nation and against God. Even then, most were thinking of disposing of Charles I the man (whether by deposing him or executing him) rather than abolishing the monarchy as such. The prince of Wales was out of the question, but could an alternative king be found in one of Charles's younger sons, James, duke of York, or Henry, duke of Gloucester?

In retrospect, it is difficult to imagine the extent to which the events of December 1648 and January 1649 were uncertain and contingent. Even among the senior officers there was no agreement on the fate of the king. Fairfax had opposed the Newport talks in the previous autumn, but he did not want the king to be tried, while Cromwell wanted a trial, but not necessarily the death penalty. What may finally have tipped the balance was news that Ormond was close to signing a new treaty with the Catholic Irish – and thus creating not only a security threat but also the final proof of Charles's perfidy. At the end of December, the grim mood was reflected in a sermon to the Commons, delivered by the radical minister Thomas Brook. He chose as his text Numbers 35, v.33: 'Ye shall not pollute the land wherein ye are; for the blood it defileth the land, and the land cannot be cleansed of the blood that is shed therein, but by the blood of him that shed it'.

**Figure 4** Contemporary German print depicting the execution of Charles I outside the Banqueting House, Whitehall, Westminster, 1649.

The Commons passed the ordinance creating the high court of justice for the trial of the king on 1 January 1649, but it was rejected by the Lords. This brought constitutional matters to a head, provoking the Commons to pass a resolution in which they claimed to be able to act with sovereign power, as the elected representative of the people, without the need for the assent of the lords, or of the king. The way was now clear for the appointment of commissioners for the trial on 6 January, with John Bradshaw acting as judge and John Cook as solicitor.

The public trial of the king was a piece of political theatre, at which his accusers intended to demonstrate their own authority, as well as the guilt of the king. However, Charles refused to play his part. In the proceedings that followed, he refused to accept the authority of the court, or to enter a plea; and by doing so he not only threw the trial into turmoil, but also prevented any possible settlement that might have saved his life. The king was sentenced to death on 27 January. Two days later, fifty-nine commissioners signed his death warrant.

Charles was executed outside the Banqueting House in Whitehall on 30 January. On the scaffold, he addressed his people for the last time. He warned them that their future 'liberty and freedom' depended on traditional, legitimate government, and he described himself as a martyr for this right order. He also upheld the Church of England, and thereby refuted any suggestion that he was a secret Roman Catholic. The crowd that had gathered to watch was sombre. Lines of soldiers kept the people well away from the scaffold, but it was still possible to see what followed; and, according to one eye-witness, the fall of the axe was met with 'such a groan as I never heard before, and desire I may never hear again'.

## CHARLES I'S SPEECH ON THE SCAFFOLD

Truly I desire their [the people's] liberty and freedom as much as anybody whomsoever; but I must tell you their liberty and freedom consists in having of government, those laws by which their life and their goods may be most their own. It is not for having a share in government. Sir, that is nothing pertaining to them. A subject and a sovereign are clear different things.

If I would have given way to an arbitrary way, to have all laws changed according to the power of the sword, I needed not to have come here, and therefore I tell you...that I am the martyr of the people.

I die a Christian according to the profession of the Church of England, as I found it left me by my father...I have a good cause, and I have a gracious God. I will say no more.

Source: C.V. Wedgwood, *Trial of Charles I* (World Books, London, 1964), 191–2.

# 4

# The commonwealth, 1649–51

## The royalist dilemma

The execution of King Charles I changed the whole nature of the royalist cause. The stiff formality of the court, the deeply unpopular religious changes, the defeats and humiliations of the civil war: all were forgotten in a groundswell of support for the monarchy in the early months of 1649. Shortly after the regicide, there appeared the *Eikon Basilike* – 'the royal image' – which was purported to have been written by the martyred king himself. In essence, this was a justification of the king's actions during his rule, and an assertion of the sacred authority of kings in general. This was exactly what the public wanted: the *Eikon* ran to thirty-five editions in its first year. Others followed suit, with courtiers and royalist gentlemen producing volumes of poetry, of variable quality, eulogizing the executed king. Some even drew parallels between the sufferings of the king and those of Christ. As one poet put it, 'Whitehall must be, lately his palace, now his Calvary'. There was also a market for Caroline memorabilia, whether handkerchiefs or other items dipped in his blood, or engravings and woodcuts, miniatures and playing cards. Monarchy had never been so revered.

Despite the obvious support for his cause in England, the young Charles II was not in the best position to benefit from it.

In January 1649, he was the guest of his Dutch brother-in-law, William II of Orange, but he could not hope for help from the Netherlands, which was recovering from the Thirty Years War, and had no wish to enter into another costly engagement – especially if it meant tackling the New Model Army on home ground. Nor, despite their blandishments, and the optimism of the widowed queen, Henrietta Maria, were the French likely to give substantive aid to the young king.

The best chance of regaining the throne by force lay in Ireland and Scotland. The royalist lord lieutenant of Ireland, the marquess of Ormond, had managed to make a peace of sorts between the royalists and the more moderate Catholics in Ireland a few days before the regicide, and this promised to give Charles II a base from which to invade England. The Scots had proclaimed Charles king of 'Great Britain' immediately after his father's death – a provocative act that angered the English republicans and raised the hopes of those around the king. Yet the price of active support was high, as the Scots insisted that the new king must preside over a Presbyterian nation, and take the Solemn League and Covenant himself.

The choice of policies once again split the royal councillors. The queen, supported by Henry Jermyn, Lord Percy, and others, favoured a Scottish alliance with French support. This was vigorously opposed by a group centred on Sir Edward Hyde and Lord Hopton, who saw any deal with the Presbyterians as a betrayal of the Anglican Church, and instead recommended an Irish solution, with Ormond as the crucial leader, and concessions to Catholics a necessary evil.

Charles, who did not share his father's religious or political scruples, was happy to keep his options open. He held talks with a Scottish delegation in the spring of 1649, but made no firm commitments to them, while at the same time encouraging Ormond. If the Irish plan failed, he would always be able to reopen negotiations with the Presbyterians. For Charles, the

English throne was the prize; the means to that end were not of great importance.

## Creating a British republic

In England, the dramatic events of December 1648 and January 1649 were not followed by the far-reaching revolution that some hoped for and many feared. Even the dismantling of the old system of government was very slow. It was not until 7 February 1649 that the Rump Parliament (so-called because it was only the rump or remnant of the Long Parliament) set up an executive body, to fulfil those functions traditionally performed by the king and his councillors, and, more recently, by a plethora of committees acting under parliamentary authority during the civil wars. This council of state played an important role in controlling the armed forces, and was the focus for diplomacy and foreign policy, but it was firmly under Parliament's thumb: most of the members were MPs; they were elected by Parliament annually; and their decisions were subject to parliamentary scrutiny. The establishment of an executive was followed by a great deal of constitutional tidying up. In mid-March, acts were finally passed for the abolition of the monarchy and the House of Lords, and it was not until early May that the Rump parliament voted through another crucial measure – the act declaring England to be 'a commonwealth and free state'. This last act perhaps typifies the halting, ad hoc nature of the 'English Revolution'. It consisted of only 105 words, and made no mention of what the republican state might look like – except for the brief comment that it would include neither a monarch nor an upper House of Parliament.

The main reason for this apparent reluctance to make positive statements about the new commonwealth was the sense of uncertainty within the Rump Parliament itself. Pride's Purge had not only removed the Presbyterians and crypto-royalists, but it

## AN ACT DECLARING ENGLAND TO BE A COMMONWEALTH, 19 MAY 1649

Be it declared and enacted by this present parliament, and by the authority of the same, that the people of England, and of all the dominions and territories thereunto belonging, are and shall be, and are hereby constituted, made, established and confirmed, to be a commonwealth and free state, and shall from henceforth be governed as a commonwealth and free state by the supreme authority of this nation, the representatives of the people in parliament, and by such as they shall appoint and constitute as officers and ministers under them for the good of the people, and that without any king or House of Lords.

Source: Gardiner, *The Constitutional Documents of the Puritan Revolution, 1625–1660* (3rd edition, Oxford, Clarendon Press, 1906), 388.

had also caused the voluntary withdrawal of a large number of less partisan MPs, shocked and dismayed by the army's actions. In the weeks after the Purge, only around seventy MPs attended the Commons. No more than forty of these were in any sense committed republicans, including Thomas Scot, Henry Marten, and Thomas Chaloner – and by no means were all of these men friends of the army. Aware that the Rump's legitimacy was under question, the surviving MPs were keen to persuade their former colleagues to return to the House, and gradually those opposed to the regicide – including such republican critics of the army as Sir Henry Vane and Sir Arthur Hesilrige – were coaxed back to Westminster. By February, there were further concessions, aimed at winning over the more moderate MPs secluded at Pride's Purge, with the only condition being the signing of a 'dissent', disowning the Newport Treaty with the late king. Such moves certainly provided a more respectable membership of around 200 (although only around a quarter of these men were present at any one time); but it also brought in yet more conservative MPs, who were keen to limit the power of the army in the commonwealth's affairs, and who opposed radical reform in church and state.

The slow pace of constitutional reform was matched by a lack of enthusiasm for innovation in other areas. Any major changes to Parliament were resisted, and, even when a new system was proposed in January 1650, it only involved recruiting new MPs to the existing Parliament. The creaking legal system, which was cumbersome and expensive, was defended by the lawyers in the House, who managed to prevent any serious attempt at reform during the Rump Parliament. Religious reform was also controversial. While a handful of radicals called for an abolition of church hierarchies and even the removal of a dedicated ministry and the closure of the universities, and others supported some kind of freedom for the various sects, a sizeable minority of MPs looked for a completion of the Presbyterian system first proposed by the Westminster Assembly in the mid-1640s. It is telling that the establishment of a new national church, along Presbyterian lines, was only narrowly defeated in the Commons in August 1649. Stalemate ensued, and an uneasy hybrid system evolved, with different denominations coexisting. Parliament limited itself to arranging the funding of ministers and ensuring that blasphemy and other matters, formerly the remit of the church courts, were incorporated into the common law system.

The only two areas that brought major change during the commonwealth period were the reform of the navy – which gradually became one of the strongest in Europe – and the sale of the estates of the crown, the church, and leading royalists. The former encouraged both trade and the growth of colonies in the Americas, and the latter was something of a priority for MPs, who welcomed the opportunity of buying up lands at bargain prices. A mark of the basic conservatism of the regime can be seen in its political culture. Some MPs – especially men like Chaloner and Algernon Sidney – emphasized the similarities between the current situation and that of classical Rome, and they were backed up by the arguments of writers and theorists such as Marchamont Nedham and John Milton. But most supporters of the regime were more comfortable with arguments based on the 'common good', reinforced by a repackaging of royal symbolism, ranging from the coins in people's pockets to the decorations on the warships that patrolled the seas. Everywhere, the new commonwealth coat of arms – a cross of St George conjoined with the harp of Ireland – proclaimed that the new republic was stable, traditional, and respectable.

The stolidity of the Rump parliament naturally provoked a reaction from those who had hoped for more. The Levellers, who had apparently found common ground with some within the army in the winter of 1648–9, thought they had been betrayed. Their original manifesto, *The Agreement of the People*, as revised in the dying days of 1648 by Henry Ireton and other officers, would have broadened the franchise, given extensive religious liberty, and laid down stricter rules for the separation of the army, the council of state, and the parliament. But amid the confusion of the regicide this manifesto became a political liability for the army, and was quietly dropped. The Leveller leaders reacted with fury, denouncing the bad faith of the army, and in February 1649 John Lilburne published the inflammatory pamphlet *England's New Chains Discovered*, which attacked both the senior officers and the Rump parliament politicians.

The rank and file in the army, influenced by Leveller ideas, were also on the brink of revolt in this period. Courts martial suppressed unrest, and one trooper, Robert Lockyer, was executed. His funeral in London in April became a mass demonstration, with 4,000 mourners wearing green – the Leveller colour – following the coffin. Further disturbances in May prompted swift action from Fairfax and Cromwell, and the mutiny of the army Levellers was crushed at Burford in Oxfordshire, with three of the ringleaders being executed by firing squad in the churchyard. The extent to which the army mutiny was inspired by Leveller ideas is open to question. Rather than pushing for a radical political programme, the key complaint of the troops was pay, which was seriously in arrears, and this was compounded by the unpopularity of service in the new expedition to Ireland. In fact, both these problems would soon be resolved by Parliament's decision to put all its resources into the new campaign, and to give overall command to the charismatic Oliver Cromwell.

## Cromwell in Ireland, 1649–50

When Cromwell was first nominated as Parliament's lord lieutenant of Ireland, in mid-March, he was considered the obvious man for the job. His service as a cavalry commander in the first civil war had been impressive, and his success in the second civil war – and in particular his spectacular victory against the Scots at Preston – had made him a national hero. Cromwell had wisely held aloof from Pride's Purge in December 1648, and, although he had supported the regicide and signed the death warrant in January 1649, he was able to use his popularity to persuade wavering MPs to rejoin the Rump Parliament in the following spring.

It was perhaps his concern for the delicate political situation in England that caused him to hesitate before accepting the Irish posting. His subsequent acceptance of the job was probably influenced by his intimate knowledge of the situation in Ireland, which he had followed closely since the very start of the rebellion there in October 1641. Cromwell had been a keen advocate of the 'adventure' scheme of 1642, which encouraged investment in the reconquest of Ireland in return for a share in the lands to be confiscated from the rebels; he had been a candidate as lord lieutenant in 1646, and as leader of a new force planned in 1647; and in 1648 he had again been put forward as a possible general in Ireland. At each stage, English politics had intervened to prevent significant military interventions, and the Irish Protestants, who had held out valiantly since the very beginning of the rising, were not a central part of the various plans. In 1649, Cromwell was determined to avoid repeating the mistakes of the past. He would not accept the Irish command without firm promises from Parliament that he would have full powers to conduct the campaign, with adequate financial and material support from England. And he did his best to coordinate his own plans with those of the existing commanders on the ground, taking advice from Irish Protestant refugees, and designing his campaign so that he, and they, could be supported by land and supplied by sea.

Cromwell's successful landing at Dublin on 15 August was in large part due to one of these Irish Protestant commanders – Lieutenant-General Michael Jones, the governor of the Irish capital. Jones had been besieged for several weeks by the king's lord lieutenant, the marquess of Ormond. Ormond, who had managed to cobble together a treaty between the royalists and the majority of the Catholic 'Confederation' in January 1649, was in a fairly strong military position. Already Drogheda and Dundalk, to the north, had fallen to his troops. Jones turned the tables on 2 August, when a surprise attack on an outlying royalist fort led to a major engagement, and the complete defeat of Ormond at Rathmines. The battle not only ruined Ormond's field army, it also caused a political crisis. As the marquess told a close ally, 'no thing in the defeat [is] so terrible to one as the dejection it brings upon the best inclined, and the advantage it gives to the others to work upon the fears of the people'. Ormond was thinking of the Irish Catholics, who now questioned the wisdom of joining the royalist cause; but his remarks applied equally to the Protestant royalists, who began to see the Cromwellian invasion as something to be embraced, rather than resisted.

Once the bridgehead at Dublin had been established, Cromwell had two initial aims. The first was to capture the ports on the east coast of Ireland, and to make contact with the Protestant forces in the northern province of Ulster. The second was to march south and west, to retake the Protestant enclave in Munster, which was under the control of Ormond's lieutenant, Lord Inchiquin. It was in pursuit of this strategy that Cromwell at first marched north, to tackle the royalist stronghold of Drogheda. Drogheda was protected by its medieval walls, and had recently been reinforced by Ormond, who had installed a new governor, the veteran English soldier Sir Arthur Aston. Aston refused Cromwell's summons on 10 September, and the lord lieutenant proceeded to bombard the town with siege guns brought by sea. The breach was defended furiously, but in vain, and almost the entirety of the royalist garrison – around 3,000 men, Irish and English alike – were butchered in the hours that followed. Cromwell may have expressed regret for this, but his letter to the Speaker makes it clear that the massacre was on his orders, as an example to other towns that might be tempted to resist him.

### CROMWELL'S OFFICIAL REPORT AFTER THE SIEGE OF DROGHEDA, SEPTEMBER 1649

The guns, after some two or three hundred shots, beat down the corner tower, and opened two reasonable good breaches in the east and south wall. Upon Tuesday the 10th of this instant, about five o'clock in the evening, we began the storm, and after some hot dispute we entered about seven or eight hundred men, the enemy disputing it very stiffly with us.

The enemy retreated, divers of them, into the Mill Mount: a place very strong and difficult of access, being exceedingly high, having a good graft, and strongly pallisaded. The governor, Sir Arthur Aston, and divers considerable officers being there, our men getting up to them, were ordered by me to put them all to the sword. And indeed, being in the heat of action, I forbade them to spare any that were in arms in the town, and, I think, that night they put to the sword about 2,000 men.

I am persuaded that this is a righteous judgement of God upon these barbarous wretches, who have imbrued their hands in so much innocent blood, and that it will tend to prevent the effusion of blood for the future, which are the satisfactory grounds to such actions, which otherwise cannot but work remorse and regret.

Source: W.C. Abbott, *The Writings and Speeches of Oliver Cromwell* (4 volumes, New Haven, Harvard UP), ii. 126–7.

Cromwell's grim calculation was only partially successful, as the Irish Catholics now saw their very existence under threat, and the war soon dissolved into a series of long and arduous sieges. Immediately after the capture of Drogheda, Cromwell sent a force north, under Colonel Robert Venables, to take control of the Ulster ports, and join with the Irish Protestant force at Londonderry, under Sir Charles Coote. The main army turned south, targeting the naval base of Wexford. The taking of this town led to another notorious massacre, as the English troops ran wild – this time against the wishes of their commander, who was close to agreeing surrender terms when the fighting started. The neighbouring town of New Ross gave up without a fight, but the city of Waterford refused to capitulate, leading to an indecisive siege. As the winter drew in, and his troops fell sick, Cromwell withdrew to the west, where he was welcomed by Cork and the other Munster towns, which had defected to the commonwealth in the autumn.

By the winter of 1649–50, Cromwell had achieved much of what he had set out to do. Apart from Waterford, he had control of the coast from Londonderry round to Cork. His opponents were demoralized, and the unsteady alliance between Ormond and the Irish Catholics was close to fracturing, while the Protestants had flocked to join the English. In the spring, Cromwell was able to advance inland, capturing the important city of Kilkenny in March, and then moving southwards to Clonmel, on the River Suir, where he received a major reverse.

The Irish commander, Hugh Dubh O'Neill, did not surrender once a breach was made in the town walls. Instead, he put his men to work building an earthwork behind the breach, and lined it with musketeers and cannons. As the Cromwellian troops entered the town, they found themselves in a killing zone. Perhaps 1,500 men were killed. Cromwell, appalled at the carnage, offered easy terms, and the town surrendered; but not before O'Neill and his troops had slipped away in the night.

Clonmel was Cromwell's last action in Ireland, as he was recalled to England to command a new war against the Scots at the end of May. The conclusion of the war was left to others. Henry Ireton, who now took the command as Cromwell's lord deputy, proceeded to besiege the city of Limerick, which eventually fell in October 1651; Coote, having destroyed the last of the Catholic field armies at Scarrifhollis in June 1650, moved south to invest Galway, which fell in April 1652. The end was protracted and bloody, but in political terms it was a mere sideshow. Any hope that Ireland might be the springboard for the restoration of Charles II had gone long before Cromwell arrived in London in the early summer of 1650, and the young king had already turned his attentions to securing an alliance with the Scots.

# Cromwell and the Scots, 1650–1

When the Scottish delegation returned to Charles II's court at Breda in the Low Countries in March 1650, they found a king who was at last prepared to take the Covenant, although there were still grave doubts as to his sincerity. As one contemporary put it, 'we knew from clear and demonstrable reasons, that he hated it in his heart'. In many ways, the Scots were trapped by their own covenanted logic, for the Solemn League and Covenant had guaranteed the monarchy as well as the Kirk, and they were duty bound to try to ensure the prosperity of both. Despite the misgivings of many, Charles took ship for Scotland in June, and signed the Covenant before disembarking. There were immediate tensions between the king and his royalist entourage and the so-called 'Kirk party', who had never trusted the new king's intentions towards the Scottish church or its Covenant, and were suspicious of the English courtiers who surrounded him. The king refused to send away his friends, however, and began to interfere with the raising of a new army, by trying to garner popular support for the monarchy among the troops. Eventually, he was asked to leave Edinburgh altogether, and the Kirk party purged the army of its pro-royalist elements – thus weakening the chance of mounting a successful defence of the Scottish capital against the English army.

The English council of state had resolved to invade Scotland in June 1650. The lord general, Sir Thomas Fairfax, was unwilling to lead an expedition against Parliament's old ally, and resigned his post. Cromwell was appointed lord general in his place, and began to make preparations for the new campaign in the next few weeks. His vanguard crossed the Scottish border on 22 July. What they found was a wilderness. David Leslie, the Scottish general, had taken all the food from the border area, and forced all the people to leave their homes. The Scottish forces had been withdrawn to Edinburgh, where earthwork defences had been built around the city, stretching as far as the port of Leith on the Firth of Forth.

Throughout August, Cromwell probed these defences, hoping to find a weak point, or, better still, to provoke Leslie into marching out to meet him in the field. But Leslie would not stir. The weather was bad; the troops fell ill; the supply of food and ammunition by ship was irregular. By the end of the month, the English had little choice but to retire along the coast, 'the provisions of our army being once more near exhausted and gone, the nights cold, the ground wet, the bloody flux and other diseases prevailing in the army, and the Scots hitherto refusing to fight'. Worse was to follow.

As Cromwell established a base at the little port of Dunbar, and began to evacuate his sick troops, the Scottish army, which outnumbered the English by two to one, at last made its move, bypassing the town and forming up on Doon Hill to the south-east, blocking the road to England. On 2 September, the Scots moved down the hill, closer to Dunbar, and battle became inevitable. Rather than be caught at a disadvantage, Cromwell decided to make a pre-emptive strike, hitting the right flank of the Scots and forcing it back before the rest of the army could come to its aid. The result was a collapse of Scottish morale, and the disintegration of the army, as men tried in vain to escape back to Edinburgh. Three thousand Scots were killed and ten thousand taken prisoner. In the days that followed, Leslie abandoned Edinburgh, and withdrew to strongholds north of the River Forth, including the mighty castle of Stirling.

A triumphant Cromwell saw this victory, snatched from defeat, as the clearest sign yet that God was on the side of the

---

### CROMWELL'S LETTER TO THE SPEAKER OF THE COMMONS AFTER THE BATTLE OF DUNBAR, 4 SEPTEMBER 1650

It is easy to say, the Lord hath done this. It would do you good to see and hear our poor foot go up and down making their boast of God. But, Sir, it is in your hands, and by these eminent mercies God puts it more into your hands, to give Him glory...We that serve you beg of you not to own us, but God alone; we pray you own His people more and more, for they are the chariots and horsemen of Israel. Disown yourselves, but own your authority, and improve it to curb the proud and the insolent, such as would disturb the tranquillity of England...relieve the oppressed, hear the groans of poor prisoners in England; be pleased to reform the abuses of all professions; and if there be any one that makes many poor to make a few rich, that suits not a commonwealth. If He that strengthens your servants to fight, pleases to give you hearts to set upon these things, in order to His glory, and the glory of your commonwealth, besides the benefit England shall feel thereby, you shall shine forth to other nations, who shall emulate the glory of such a pattern, and through the power of God turn into the like.

Source: Abbott, *Writings and Speeches*, ii. 324–5.

commonwealth, and he told the Rump Parliament, in no uncertain terms, that serious political and religious reforms must follow.

The great victory at Dunbar was followed by a period of stalemate. Cromwell's hopes that it would bring the fall of Scotland, and important changes in England, proved to be premature. The Scots were more divided than ever, with the radical covenanters of the south-west even considering making peace with the enemy rather than continuing to associate with their ungodly king. The purged royalists flooded back to the Scottish army, and, in a show of defiance, Charles was crowned as king at Scone on 1 January 1651. The English army had consolidated its position south of the Forth, but could not make a breakthrough to the north, partly because Cromwell fell ill in the early months of 1651.

It was only in July that the position changed, as John Lambert managed to force a crossing of the Firth, and to defeat a Scottish force at Inverkeithing in Fife. A swift march north followed, with Perth falling in August. Just as the Scottish situation looked irretrievable, Charles II and his advisers decided on a last gamble – to abandon the north and march into England. This bold stroke seems to have caught the English off-guard. The council of state panicked. Thomas Harrison was quickly sent north to gather troops and raise the militia, in an attempt to keep the Scots away from London. Lambert turned south, to shadow the Scots as they marched through Lancashire and Cheshire, and Cromwell followed with the main army. Yet Charles's hopes of raising the northern royalists, and of making contact with his friends in Wales came to nothing, and he was eventually forced to halt his footsore troops at Worcester.

The last battle of the English Civil Wars took place at Worcester. Any hope of the royalists marching on to London vanished once Cromwell had reached Evesham on 25 August, effectively blocking the road east. Other English forces were soon stationed to the west of the Severn, preventing the Scots from retreating into the pro-royalist Welsh marches. Some around the king counselled that it was still possible for the cavalry to break out, and for the king to escape. When news of this reached the already disillusioned Scottish infantry, there was near mutiny. Their commanders were also divided. David Leslie, the most experienced of the Scottish commanders, found his advice ignored; the English duke of Buckingham, who believed he should be the overall commander, refused to obey the commands of others; and Charles was surrounded by flatterers and optimists, including the unstable 2nd duke of Hamilton. It seemed that, even after nine years of struggle, the royalists had still not managed to put aside their personal differences and unite behind their king.

It was a very different picture in the Cromwellian camp. There was no question who was in charge. Cromwell was not only lord general, but he was also a charismatic political leader of shrewd judgement, who knew how to inspire his men, and when to trust his subordinates. When the attack on Worcester came, it had the hallmarks of a Cromwellian campaign. Having rested his troops for a week, Cromwell chose 3 September – the anniversary of his dramatic victory at Dunbar the year before – to commit his men. The initial approach was carefully timed, as bridges of boats needed to be constructed across the Severn and the Teme to ensure troops could be switched from one side of the city to the other.

When it at last came, the attack was led by a trusted lieutenant, Charles Fleetwood, who forced the Scots out of the village of Powick and pushed them back into the city. Immediately afterwards, two more of Cromwell's protégés, John Lambert and Thomas Harrison, staunchly resisted a desperate attack from the Scots, sallying from the western gate of the city – an attack that crumbled when Cromwell led his reserve into their flank. The defeated forces fled back into the suburbs; Fort Royal was taken; and soon the New Model Army was within the city walls. In the ensuing chaos, the duke of Hamilton was mortally wounded, David Leslie reputedly 'rode up and down as one amazed, or

**A SCOTTISH REACTION TO NEWS OF THE BATTLE OF WORCESTER, SEPTEMBER 1651**

I heard the king and 3,000 horse was taken, as we had heard before of the duke of Hamilton and [earl of] Rothes and 7,000 prisoners.

I remembered that I said often…that if they let the king go in the head of the army, his head, I feared, would go with it.

This night we heard again of 10,000 prisoners, 647 officers, all their colours, bag and baggage and [artillery] train taken, which is a strange thing to think upon; and it is as strange, if it be true, what some report – that they will bring king and lords to Scotland, there to be executed.

Source: *Diary of Sir Archibald Johnston of Wariston, volume ii, 1650–4*, ed. D.H. Fleming (Edinburgh, 1919), 135–6.

seeking to fly he knew not whither', and Charles II managed to escape with some of the cavalry. As many as three thousand Scots lay dead; a further seven thousand were taken prisoner. The royalist cause had been completely destroyed.

The parliamentarians were elated by the victory. Remembering that the first skirmish of the civil wars had happened at Powick Bridge on 23 September 1642, the New Model Army chaplain, Hugh Peter, gave an almost Shakespearean oration to the militia regiments immediately after Worcester: 'when your wives and children shall ask you where you have been, and what news; say you have been at Worcester, where England's sorrows began, and where they are happily ended'.

# Aftermath

The defeat of Charles II at Worcester may have brought the civil wars to an end, but it did not solve the problems of mid-seventeenth-century England. Oliver Cromwell was now the most powerful figure in the country, but he was not able to implement a radical reform programme because of resistance from the mainly conservative MPs in the Rump Parliament. When Cromwell returned to London after Worcester, there were high hopes that something truly revolutionary might be about to happen. Cromwell himself had written to Parliament, immediately after the battle, that God had shown his favour to 'the nation and the change of government', and now expected that 'justice and righteousness, mercy and truth may flow from you, as a thankful return to our gracious God'.

A few weeks later, the radical author and leader of the 'Diggers', Gerrard Winstanley, was encouraged to hope for a brave new world, urging Cromwell to consider a radical new constitution that would bring equality and the redistribution of land, and saying that 'a man must either be a free and true commonwealth's man, or a monarchical tyrannical royalist'. Winstanley was over-optimistic. The Cromwell who had argued against, and then destroyed, the Levellers was not ready for social revolution. His main aim was a religious transformation, backed by the power of the New Model Army, and he was intent on trying to persuade Parliament to support this. Their reticence and foot-dragging led to confrontation and, eventually, to the forced closure of the Rump parliament in April 1653 and the creation of 'the rule of the saints' by a new council of state and a 'Nominated Assembly', soon christened 'Barebone's Parliament' after one of its more radical members. This experiment in godly rule proved a dismal failure, and it was dissolved in December 1653, when Cromwell, influenced by senior army officers, became head of state as lord protector. This new government was compromised by its reliance on the army, which cut across efforts by Cromwell and others to reconcile old enemies – whether moderate royalists or Presbyterians – in a process known as 'healing and settling'.

Cromwell's reluctance to reduce the influence of the army left a very difficult legacy for his son, Richard, who succeeded as protector on Oliver's death in September 1658. In April 1659,

Richard faced a military coup, and resigned as protector a month later, and England faced a series of short-lived governments over the following year: the restored Rump parliament; a military junta; the Rump parliament again; and finally a council of state and a Convention, which agreed to negotiate the unconditional return of King Charles II in May 1660.

# 5
# The armies

The apparently inexorable narrative of the political crisis known as the 'English Revolution' helps to convey much of the excitement and bewilderment of the two decades in the middle of the seventeenth century. But there is also a need to focus on particular issues that do not lend themselves to narrative treatment. What were the great battles like, and what were the qualities needed to command armies and win great victories? In what ways did political thought, and religious ideas, develop during these years? And what was the experience of those caught up in the military, political, and religious turmoil – the civilian population, who became active participants in events, as well as the victims of them? It is perhaps appropriate to start with the nuts and bolts: the experience of the junior officers and ordinary soldiers 'going to the wars'.

## Raising troops

When political crisis became open civil war in the late summer of 1642, the opposing generals faced one major problem: England was perhaps the least warlike nation in Europe. Aside from periodic, and generally disorganized, local rebellions, there had been no armed conflict within England since the end of the Wars of the Roses 150 years before. Even the Reformation, though bitterly resented by many, had not resulted in the kind of civil war that erupted in France and the Netherlands in the second half of the sixteenth century. The Tudors had taken care to reduce the regional influence of the nobility by increasing the power of the state. In response, ambitious aristocrats became courtiers rather than warlords, they conducted their disputes through the law courts, and stately homes replaced defensible castles. The only standing forces available to the crown were the yeomen of the guard at the Tower of London and the gentlemen pensioners, who formed the monarch's bodyguard. Internal security depended instead on the militia forces, part-time soldiers of questionable quality who mustered in each county under a noble lord lieutenant and his gentry deputies. Whether these troops would have stood for long against Spanish veterans was thankfully never put to the test; and, as the Armada scare of 1588 demonstrated, in truth, England's safety depended on the Channel, the Royal Navy, and the weather.

In the early seventeenth century, England's military reputation sank to a new low, as James I refused to become embroiled in the Thirty Years War (1618–48) on the continent. Charles I, egged on by his favourite, the duke of Buckingham, embarked on a series of disastrous expeditions against Spain and France in the 1620s, and then signed an ignominious peace with both countries in 1629. Apart from these occasional forays, the only chance for Englishmen to follow the drum was to serve in foreign armies. The Thirty Years War saw the recruitment of entire units from Ireland and Scotland (both countries with a stronger martial tradition – and greater lawlessness – than England), and there were opportunities for gentlemen from all three Stuart kingdoms to join the officer corps of the rival armies. Sir Jacob Astley, who commanded the royalist foot at Edgehill, had served in Flanders and Germany; Sir Arthur Aston, the defender of Drogheda, had seen service in the armies of Russia, Poland, and Sweden; the New Model Army's lord general, Sir Thomas Fairfax, had fought in France and Poland. These, and many others who quickly returned from the foreign wars, formed the leaven in the lump of amateur soldiers who found themselves thrown into civil war in 1642.

Even though there was a nucleus of experienced officers avail-able to both sides at the outbreak of war, the forming of armies was a massive task. The militia units were the obvious source for recruiting serjeants, but these suffered from lack of training and experience of war, and even the legality of mobilizing them was uncertain. The king resorted to a long-defunct medieval order, known as the 'commission of array', to raise the local forces in his defence. Parliament passed its own 'militia ordinance', author-izing gentry committees to raise troops, but without the king's assent everyone knew this was not a proper statute. Neither ploy was a resounding success. Charles had mustered barely a thousand men when he raised his standard at Nottingham in August 1642, and he soon came to rely on individual commissions to colonels to raise regiments of volunteers. These men were drawn mainly from Wales and the west midlands, the north-west (especially Lancashire), and the south-west (notably Cornwall).

When conflict and desertion had severely depleted these regi-ments of volunteers, the king fell back on conscription, a process well in train by the summer of 1644. Parliament had pressed men into the ranks from the beginning, but they also relied on the London militia or 'trained bands', and on the efforts of individu-als to raise volunteer regiments in eastern England, especially the home counties and East Anglia. By these methods, relatively large armies could be brought to battle. It has been estimated that both sides fielded 12,000 men at Edgehill in 1642; at Marston Moor in 1644 – certainly the largest battle of the civil wars – as many as 18,000 royalists fought 28,000 parliamentarians; and at Naseby in 1645 the king had no more than 12,500 men, while the New Model Army numbered perhaps 17,000.

To these field armies must be added innumerable local forces and garrisons of urban areas, castles, and other outposts scattered across the country, and dependent on their neighbours for food and other supplies. The devolved nature of warfare served to blur the already indistinct boundaries between soldiers and civilians, and the old militia regiments needed encouragement to move across their county boundaries. The Cornish levy refused to move into Devon in 1643, and even the motivated London-trained bands resisted attempts to march them away from the capital.

The seasonal nature of warfare (with very little fighting happening during the winter months, when the roads were all but impassable) meant that for many the war was at best a part-time venture. Royalist infantry regiments came near to disbanding altogether in the winter, as soldiers headed for home, and the same could happen in Parliament's armies. The forces under the earl of Essex dropped by two thirds in the months following Edgehill, but had returned to full strength when war resumed in April 1643. Even the New Model Army, renowned for its discipline, was dogged by absenteeism, with around 4,000 foot soldiers disappearing after the victory at Naseby. The overall impression is that, although England was engaged in a lengthy, and bloody, civil war, few of the amateurs entirely shook off their deep-rooted civilian ways. It was only with the professionalization of warfare, after the creation of the New Model Army in 1645, that a military caste began to emerge.

## Battles and sieges

The armies of the civil wars would have appeared slightly shambolic to modern eyes, used to the precise drill of Trooping the Colour or Victorian paintings of the Battle of Waterloo. The basic unit, whether of cavalry or infantry was the regiment, commanded by a colonel, with lieutenant-colonel, major and several captains in command of companies or troops, but, while these top jobs were usually filled, the number of ordinary soldiers could vary wildly. Regiments were routinely broken up, with companies or troops assigned to other duties, and many were seriously under-strength. Notionally, the New Model Army regiment of foot was made up of 1,200 men, with cavalry regiments having 600 troopers, but it was rare that the full complement reached the field. At Naseby, the typical New Model Army regiment of foot numbered around 800 men, while the horse regiments were no more than 500 strong. In the same battle, royalist regiments were very weak, with even the largest, Prince Rupert's bluecoats, having no more than 500 other ranks, while the largest regiment of horse, Colonel Vaughan's, had perhaps 400 troopers. As the war continued, some royalist units came close to disappearing altogether. During the last, desperate days of the siege of Pendennis in the spring of 1646, Colonel Tremaine's regiment was reduced to nine officers and forty-eight men. In the circumstances, it is hardly surprising that regiments were amalgamated on the battlefield, to create units of a sensible size, even at the expense of regimental esprit de corps.

Morale may also have been affected by a distinct lack of uniformity within the armies. In the early stages of the war, uniforms depended on the whim of the colonel, and regiments were often known by the colours chosen: the earl of Newcastle's Whitecoats, for example. This was not a problem in a small-scale action, but large battles could become chaotic, as it became increasingly difficult, amid the smoke and noise, to distinguish friend from foe. To counteract this, soldiers wore 'field signs', such as the orange scarf adopted by Essex's men, or white paper worn in the hats of parliamentarians at Marston Moor. It was the New Model Army that solved the problem, as (according to one contemporary newsbook – the equivalent to a modern-day newspaper) 'the men are redcoats all, the whole army only are distinguished by several facings of their coats'. In 1645, for the first time, English soldiers had become Redcoats.

The shortcomings of the regimental structure, and the often inadequate training given to the soldiers, explain why most civil war battles were fairly basic affairs. Invariably, infantry units were

## INFANTRY

Infantry (or 'foot') regiments comprised two basic types of soldier: the pikeman and the musketeer. Traditionally, pikemen were the tallest and strongest of the soldiers, as they had to handle a sixteen-foot-long pike, a spear used to fend off enemy cavalry and to stab at other infantry at close quarters. The pikemen were also supposed to wear heavy armour, including back-and-breast plates, tassets (which covered the thighs), and a simple iron helmet. In practice, pikemen often lightened their load by dispensing with most of this armour, often retaining only the helmet; and it was common for the men to shorten their pikes by cutting a foot or more off the end. Musketeers formed the majority of troops in civil war armies, ideally outnumbering the pikemen by two-to-one. They were usually armed with a smoothbore matchlock musket, which fired a lead ball of around an ounce in weight. These weapons were inaccurate against individual targets and at long range, but could be quite effective at distances of less than a hundred yards, especially if fired in volleys against the massed ranks of an attacking enemy. The rate of fire was slow, and often only a few rounds could be fired before hand-to-hand combat began. Like the pikemen, musketeers were usually armed with a basic sword, but in close fighting they tended to use the iron-bound butt of the musket as a very effective club instead.

marshalled with a block of pikemen in the centre with musketeers on either side. Each army would be made up of a number of these units, perhaps arranged in a chequer pattern, allowing the reserve to advance in support of the front line. Complicated manoeuvres were seldom attempted. The cavalry were also trained in the simplest of ways, using the 'Swedish' system, with units of three ranks deep advancing in close order at the trot until charging home, with the sword being the main offensive weapon. Generals mostly played safe. At Edgehill, Marston Moor, and Naseby, the armies lined up facing each other, with the infantry in the centre (in two or more lines) and the cavalry on the wings. In each case, one side attacked the other, the cavalry charging and being repulsed or, more often, disappearing in pursuit of the routed foe. The infantry came to within a few dozen yards of the enemy, firing muskets, and, after a last volley, fell on them 'at push of pike and butt end of musket'. This close-quarter struggle continued until either both sides disengaged and re-formed (as at Edgehill), or one side was pushed back in disorder. Cavalry returning to the field, or held in reserve, could prove decisive at this point, and they were certainly of great importance as the defeated army was driven from the field. As we shall see in the next chapter, not all battles followed this pattern, and there were generals of real ability who were more than capable of doing the unexpected, and snatching victory from defeat.

Battles, especially large ones, were very much the exception during the civil war. The network of rival garrisons, each surviving on the produce and plunder provided by their immediate

## CAVALRY

The dominance of the cavalry (or 'horse') in warfare had been challenged in the sixteenth century, when first pikes and then muskets made the infantry less vulnerable to armoured horsemen. By the mid-seventeenth century, battlefield armour had become less important, and cavalrymen were routinely armed with a variety of firearms as well as swords. The relic of the armoured cavalryman, known as the 'cuirassier', dressed in plate armour from head to knee, was only found in generals' lifeguards and one regiment of the parliamentarian army, Sir Arthur Hesilrige's famous 'lobsters'. Most of the cavalry were 'harquebusiers', armed with a short-barrelled carbine and a brace of pistols. These men wore either a broad-brimmed hat or a helmet and a thick leather 'buff-coat', with or without back-and-breast plates. The cavalry were primarily used as shock troops against opposing cavalry or disordered foot units. They were also essential as scouts during campaign, and as instruments of vengeance in the pursuit that inevitably followed a decisive battle. Another form of horse troops were the dragoons, mounted infantry armed with flintlock muskets, who usually fought on foot.

hinterland, led to much skirmishing and raiding. Another typical action was the siege. Again, these varied in scale. The early months of the war were marked by the seizure of ill-defended houses, the capture of towns with makeshift earthworks, and the blockading of more formidable strongholds. Some sieges could last, with varying levels of intensity, for years, but only in a few cases were formal siege works – familiar from the continental wars – laid out, and there were correspondingly few places, aside from large cities such as London, Bristol, and Oxford, that could boast 'modern' defences with bastions and extensive outworks. In most cases, medieval walls were reinforced with earth banks, and the defenders were left to hope that a relieving force would arrive soon.

## ARTILLERY

Civil war armies were equipped with a bewildering array of artillery pieces, from antiquated weapons taken from aristocratic collections to the newly cast products from the iron foundries of the Kentish Weald. There were two basic types. Field guns were small and light, rarely exceeding the 6-pounder 'saker' in calibre. These guns either fired a solid iron ball or 'case-shot', formed by packing musket balls into a metal or wooden cylinder, which would then spray the unfortunate enemy at close range. The effectiveness of field artillery is a moot point. Sometimes, as at Langport in 1645, the fire was accurate and effective; in most other battles, there was time only for a few shots before the guns were overrun. It was during sieges that artillery came into its own. Siege guns were cumbersome monsters, the largest being 48-pounder 'full cannons', and it was preferable to transport them by ship or boat if possible. They would be emplaced within a few hundred yards of the chosen target, in an attempt to blast a breach in the defences, and, as most civil war towns or castles relied on medieval stone walls, if the artillery were of sufficient size, the end was inevitable. The siege train also included large mortars, which lobbed explosive bombs over walls and caused fear and destruction in equal measure.

Often the best plan for an attacker was not to settle down for a long siege, but to create a breach and take the town by force. Basing House in Hampshire, which commanded the road to the west, was repeatedly besieged, but fell in 1645 only after bombardment by the largest guns available and a storm by the cream of the New Model foot regiments, cheered on by Oliver Cromwell. Cromwell put a similar plan into effect at Drogheda in 1649, when the strong resistance of the Irish and English force defending the town resulted in quarter being denied, and the massacre of the whole garrison. Such brutality was extremely unusual in England, where there were fairly rigidly defined rules of conduct, reflecting the sense of honour and obligation between officers who were also gentlemen.

## Officers and men

Perhaps the greatest social gulf in seventeenth-century England was between those who were accepted as gentlemen and gentlewomen and those who were not. This was not necessarily a matter of wealth alone: ancestry, education, and upbringing all played an important part in distinguishing between the haves and the have-nots. Although it was possible to rise into the ranks of the gentry (or even further), and to fall to the status of a yeoman, it was unusual for this to happen within a generation. To take a famous example, in the early 1630s, Oliver Cromwell, having sold his modest estate in Huntingdon, took the lease of a farm in neighbouring St Ives. Cromwell, the grandson of a knight, a Cambridge graduate, and a former MP (for Huntingdon in 1628–9), was not in danger of slipping socially as well as economically. The real threat was that his sons and daughters would lose their gentry status in years to come. The rigidity of the social system was replicated in the civil war armies, with the officer class thinking, and acting, in very different ways to the rank and file.

Officers were bound by strong conventions of honour, which has been defined by one historian as the sense of 'uncompromised personal integrity'. This was a complex phenomenon, including elements of polite civility to equals, due deference to superiors (including the king), and a commitment to kinship ties and to maintaining the conventions that cemented the social hierarchy. These were attitudes common to all gentlemen, but they were felt acutely by officers whose military duties often contravened such codes of behaviour. The awkwardness felt by senior officers is well known. As the parliamentarian general Sir William Waller told his old friend and new opponent Sir Ralph Hopton in 1643, 'my affections to you are so unchangeable, that hostility itself cannot violate my friendship to your person, but I must be true to the cause wherein I serve'. This can also be seen in Fairfax's praise of Hopton in 1645 as 'an honest man, a soldier and a Christian'.

Two other elements were also of the greatest importance. The first was professional pride among the officers, especially those who had served abroad, or (in later years) those who had been with the New Model Army in the glory years of 1645–6. The second was a sense of shared beliefs, whether the religious Independency of the New Model Army cavalry or the quasi-religious commitment of many royalists to King Charles. Not all officers lived up to these high ideals, of course. Some were cruel or duplicitous or morally suspect. The royalist cavalry commander George Lord Goring was the most notorious example of excess. As one contemporary put it, he 'strangely loved the bottle, was much given to pleasures, and a great debauchee'.

Ordinary soldiers were often deeply attached to their commanders, even those who fell far short of the officers' code. Thus, the debauched Goring was respected by his men, who continued to be loyal to him even in defeat. The ineffective parliamentarian general the earl of Essex was also a popular commander, helped by his common touch. In contrast, the sober and pious New

Model Army colonel of dragoons, John Okey, was a moody man disliked by his soldiers and junior officers, with one of them saying 'that he is either all honey or all shit'. But Okey had been a tallow chandler before the war, and may not have been considered a true gentleman.

The very different attitudes of the other ranks serve as a reminder that their belief system was not the same as that of the officer class. That does not mean that they had no values at all, but genuine accounts of them are difficult to recover, mostly because the records we have are either comments by their superiors or the proceedings of courts punishing crimes.

As we have seen, ordinary soldiers were often reluctant and ill-trained young men, newly released from parental and community control, and given weapons. Violence and excess were not unlikely outcomes. Yet, in many cases, disorder and moral shortcomings had causes other than an inherently criminal mentality. The lawyer Bulstrode Whitelocke, whose estates had suffered at the hands of rival armies in the mid-1640s, may have been dismissive of 'brutish soldiers, who know no difference between friends and foe, but all is plunder', but it is likely that many of these soldiers had not been paid for months. Equally, the royalist

## PAY

The rates of pay varied surprisingly little between the royalist and parliamentarian armies. What did differ was the frequency with which it was actually paid, with Parliament more likely to honour its commitments as the war continued. The basic pay for a foot soldier was eight pence a day, while a cavalry trooper received either two shillings or two shillings and sixpence. Dragoons were paid the lesser amount of one shilling and sixpence. Mounted troops were expected to pay for the upkeep of their horses from these sums, and all soldiers must have struggled to cover their costs when on campaign. This was also true of the officer class, who also had to cover the expense of servants and additional mounts and baggage horses. A captain would expect eight shillings a day, while his colonel received £1, and the commander-in-chief was usually allowed £10 a day. There was no easy way to make money from the wars, unless through plunder (either legal, following the storming of a stronghold, or illegal) or reward. Bearers of the good news of victory were rewarded by king or Parliament; and successful commanders were often granted lands, titles, or a fat pension.

press may have laughed at the Dorset soldiers who could only be induced to attack Corfe Castle when plied with drink, but the walls had not been breached and the assault was near suicidal.

As for religion, it should not be assumed that the soldiers were either uninterested or fervently committed. Even the New Model Army, the army of the 'saints', appears to have been something of a mixed bag. One hostile witness called the newly formed New Model Army 'an ungodly crew' who 'knead all their dough with ale, for I never see so many drunk in my life in so short a time'. Even Fairfax's chaplain, Joshua Sprigge, admitted to their faults, for 'armies are too great bodies to be sound in all parts at once'.

# The face of battle

So far, this account of the armies of the civil wars has been conventional. We have considered the difficulties faced by those raising armies from a non-military society, how those soldiers were organized and brought to battle, and the differences between the attitudes of the officers and men who served together. But the experience of fighting is less easy to capture. What was it actually like to be a civil war soldier? Perhaps the best way to approach this difficult topic is through a case study, following the experiences of one regiment during a short period in 1644, to try to get a flavour of military service during this period.

The soldiers of the foot regiment of Murrough O'Brien, Lord Inchiquin, were veterans of the bitter Irish wars who had been brought over in the winter of 1643–4 to assist the royalists in the south-west of England. A mixture of Irish Protestants and Catholics, they had already proved their worth in a number of skirmishes, including a bloody action in February 1644, at Holme Bridge, three miles from the parliamentarian garrison of Wareham in Dorset. Encountering 300 local parliamentarians, the Irish force, which numbered less than 50, advanced to take the bridge, and 'both officers and common men expressed most gallant courage' in a skirmish that lasted about four hours, with the soldiers giving ground only once their officers had been wounded. Surviving accounts of this action are from royalist sources, so are likely to be biased, but in their next engagement Inchiquin's men were to prove their worth beyond any doubt.

The town of Wareham, just inland from Poole Harbour, was defended by two rivers and its old Saxon walls, now refortified. In April 1644, it was attacked at night by Inchiquin's men, who scaled the walls under gunfire, climbing through 'the port-holes of the cannon while the ordnance played upon them, though they had scarce room to get betwixt the mouth of the cannon and the wall'. Once inside the town, they killed as many as 80 parliamentarians and captured 300 prisoners with their weapons, at the cost of two dead and five wounded of their own. They were not christened the 'brave Irish' and 'incomparable musketeers' by the royalist press for nothing.

By the summer, Inchiquin's men had further strengthened the defences at Wareham with gun platforms, mounting artillery pieces, including six 'murderers' designed to fire small-calibre 'hailshot' against attackers at close range, more often used on small naval vessels. They had also fortified a position in the Bestwall area outside the town walls, which commanded the approaches from Poole Harbour. It was on this side that local parliamentarians, reinforced by regular cavalry and dragoons under Waller's lieutenant-general John Middleton, attacked in force on 10 August. According to an eye-witness, 'they stormed the enemy out of Bestwall', forcing the Irish soldiers back into the town. This bald statement masks the true nature of this brief engagement, but other sources supply details.

One newsbook recounts how the senior officers were caught in heavy fire, with Middleton having 'his horse shot under him'. The accounts of the parliamentarian treasurer for Dorset include the payment of ten shillings for 'the cure of a mare of Colonel Bingham's troop hurt in fight with the Irish'. This suggests that the Irish were following contemporary best practice and aiming at the horses rather than the men. Perhaps the most poignant of the casualties was another parliamentarian, Lieutenant Thomas Butler, who led the initial line of skirmishers – the 'forlorn hope' – and for his bravery had 'both his eyes shot out'. The archaeological evidence, derived from an excavation of only part of the site, adds to the picture. Over 500 pieces of shot were discovered – suggesting that this was a bitterly fought struggle – with 15 caps from musketeers' powder flasks, finds often associated with intensive fighting. The shot varied greatly in size, with many falling into the pistol or carbine calibres (again pointing to cavalry involvement), as well as a number of musket balls. This corroborates documentary evidence showing that the local parliamentarian cavalry was armed with carbines as well as pistols.

The ferocity of the Irish troops against this determined attack made the parliamentarians think twice before mounting a further attack on the town, and it was decided to try to persuade the Irish to surrender. This was less than straightforward, because a large proportion of the Irish troops (around 140) were Irish Catholics, and the earl of Essex had recently issued a direct order to Colonel William Sydenham that such men were to be denied quarter. As Essex put it, when it came to the 'absolute Irish, you may cause them to be executed, for I would not have quarter allowed to those'. This order had been carried out at least once, and the royalists had retaliated by executing captured parliamentarians. No wonder the Irish troops had put up such a stiff resistance.

On receiving the offer of terms, there was a long debate among Inchiquin's men. Eventually, the Catholics were over-ruled by their Protestant comrades, who had no wish to suffer a long siege or another assault, and the garrison surrendered. The fate of the Irish Catholics was included in the articles of surrender, and they were treated surprisingly leniently. Maybe the local commanders had been unhappy with Essex's diktat; perhaps Middleton had feared for his own professional reputation. In any case, as one newsbook put it, 'the Irish rebel papists…were sent to Bristol without arms, according to the articles; and so many Irish women and children with them, that it is believed every soldier had his trull [whore], their number was so great'. The Irish Prot-estant troops all changed sides, enlisting with the parliamentarian army.

The case of Inchiquin's regiment is interesting because it represents the sort of actions – raids, skirmishes, and attacks on strongholds – that were typical of the first civil war. In this case, an important town had become the base for outsiders, and a thorn in the flesh of the neighbouring town. When an assault was attempted, local forces were joined by regular units in the assault, and a fierce fight ensued. The bloodshed was kept to a minimum, however, and both sides were eager to agree terms. This was a story that was replicated across England.

Yet there are also elements here that are very unusual indeed. The presence of not only Irish troops, but Irish Catholics, stirred up ethnic and religious animosities, not helped by orders from the lord general to treat the Catholic contingent as vermin. The commanders on the ground seem to have shied away from this, however, and were content merely to disarm the Catholics and send them away. Their departure revealed, almost as an after-thought, another side to military life at this time: the presence of a large number of camp followers, wives, mistresses, and children, caught up in what might have become an ugly incident. Far from home, they had no choice but to follow their men as they trudged to Bristol. The Catholics left behind their former comrades, who now enlisted for Parliament, and a number of dead and injured. What the inhabitants of Wareham thought of it all, we can only imagine.

# 6

# The generals

As the case of Inchiquin's regiment shows, much of the fighting in the early years of the civil wars was small scale, and ad hoc, with decisions being made by local commanders. Large sieges or set-piece battles were relatively rare, and they presented additional problems to the generals who conducted them. The troops in the larger field armies were often ill-trained, and in many cases had been brought together from disparate forces for a single engagement. As a result, the strategic and tactical opportunities open to the generals were limited. Indeed, it was something of an achievement to bring the enemy to battle and then to marshal the army into a basic linear formation. Once the battle started, the extent to which generals could control events was extremely limited, unless a body of men could be kept in reserve, and many commanders made their names not by giving orders but by personal courage, in the thick of the fighting.

As the civil wars continued, the armies of both sides grew more professional – both in terms of the experience of the troops and also the increased availability of money and supplies – and the opportunities for talented generals to prove themselves also grew. But there were still important limits on what could be achieved. In this chapter, we will look more closely at the nature of generalship in the period, by considering the performance of three of the most successful of the civil war generals in three separate campaigns: Prince Rupert at Marston Moor in 1644; Sir Thomas Fairfax at Naseby in 1645; and Oliver Cromwell at Preston in 1648. The aim is not to conduct a military beauty contest, to discover who the best commander might have been, but to consider how generals were able to overcome the problems inherent in early modern warfare, and to use their initiative and cunning to win crucial advantages over their foes.

## Rupert and the Marston Moor campaign, June–July 1644

The battle of Marston Moor, which took place near York on 2 July 1644, was an important victory for the enemies of the king. A combined army of Scots, Yorkshire troops under the Fairfaxes, and men from the Eastern Association (including its veteran cavalry led by Cromwell) destroyed a slightly smaller force of royalists, made up of Rupert's troops from Wales, the marches and the north-west, and the northern army of the earl of Newcastle. Militarily, Marston Moor lost the king the north of England; politically, it vindicated the Anglo-Scottish alliance, and silenced those at Westminster who called for a quick peace treaty with the king.

Marston Moor also dented the reputation of Rupert, who until then had been seen as an unstoppable, even diabolical, force. He had led the dramatic cavalry charge at Edgehill in October 1642, and swept the parliamentarian horse away; he had led the successful assault on Bristol in July 1643, showing immense personal bravery in the breach; and his latest victory, at Newark in March, had again shown how effective an aggressive attack could be. At Marston Moor, Rupert took personal charge of the shaken royalist cavalry on his right wing, and led a counter-attack, only to join the rout when the parliamentarians gained the upper hand. His actions as a general have been much criticized as a result.

**Figure 5** Prince Rupert as a young man. Portrait by Anthony van Dyck c. 1637.

In rushing to the aid of his cavalry, he had left the army without an overall commander. As one contemporary complained, 'the victory was so doubtful that, had the prince but stayed in the field to own it, the day had been ours'. Worse was to follow. Rupert not only lost the battle, but he also became separated from his men, and was forced to hide in a bean field until he could make good his escape. Yet the defeat on 2 July was not inevitable. In fact, the parliamentarians snatched victory only at the last moment, after losing, hands down, to a brilliantly planned and executed campaign, masterminded by Rupert.

Rupert is often seen as a proud and conceited man, whose position as nephew of the king made him difficult to handle. But he could be a very able military administrator – as he demonstrated in the early months of 1644, when he took over control of Wales and the marches, settling local disputes, reforming the raising of taxation, and recruiting fresh troops for local forces. He could also be cautious. He did not take to the field until the parliamentarians in south-west Wales had been defeated in May, and then he marched north into Cheshire and Lancashire, taking Liverpool and Bolton before establishing himself at Preston, but being careful not to advance too far from his supply bases.

Rupert was already developing a bolder plan, to relieve the vital royalist city of York, besieged by a mixed force of English and Scots. This stroke not only required careful military preparation, but it also needed the approval of the king. This did not come. Charles, fearing the convergence of other parliamentarian armies in an attempt on his capital at Oxford, was busy reacting to events rather than contemplating bold strokes. In the event, the

## RUPERT UNDER ORDERS. AN EXTRACT FROM THE LETTER OF CHARLES I TO RUPERT, 14 JUNE 1644

If York be lost, I shall esteem my crown little less [than lost], unless supported by your sudden march to me, and a miraculous conquest in the south before the effects of the northern power can be found here. But if York be relieved, and you beat the rebels' armies of both kingdoms which were before it – then, but not otherwise, I may possibly make a shift upon the defensive, to spin out time until you come to assist me. Wherefore I command and conjure you... that, all new enterprises laid aside, you immediately march according to your first intention, with all your force, to the relief of York.

Source: quoted in Austin Woolrych, *Battles of the English Civil War* (London, Pan Books, 1961), 57.

decision by Parliament's lord general, the earl of Essex, to march into the south-west relieved the pressure on Oxford; and Charles, who had fled to the midlands, wrote to Rupert on 14 June to encourage him to take action.

The tone of Charles's letter to Rupert was somewhat ambiguous. Charles's fearful references to the loss of his crown, his warning that only a miracle could save the royalists in the south, alarmed Rupert into thinking that he had to move fast. And, while Charles clearly expected Rupert to relieve York, it was not at all clear whether he was to bring the allies to battle at all costs, or whether such an encounter was at the prince's discretion.

Rupert, fearing the worst, prepared to march immediately, even though fresh recruits were arriving every day. From Preston in Lancashire, he crossed the Pennines to Skipton, where he met the northern horse, and pushed on to Knaresborough on 30 June. From there, he could reach the western approaches to York in less than a day. News of his rapid movement eastwards and southwards soon reached the commanders in the siege works around York, and they hastily raised the siege and marched on to Marston Moor, which commanded the roads from the west of the city. Rupert's riposte was swift and unexpected. Instead of marching straight for York, on 1 July he headed north-east, crossed the River Ouse at Boroughbridge and the River Swale at Thornton Bridge, and struck south again, reaching the unguarded eastern side of York that night. En route, he captured a pontoon bridge at Poppleton, which allowed some of his cavalry to form up between York and the Anglo-Scottish army. His footsore infantry, who had marched twenty-two miles that day, camped outside York. The city was saved; Rupert was hailed as a hero; and the king's enemies had been completely outmanoeuvred. Yet Rupert, encouraged by the king's equivocal instructions, wanted more.

Rupert's march on York had relied on speed, surprise, and unified command. On the morning of 2 July, he thought he could again rely on all three. He had been reinforcing his cavalry on the moor since dawn, and there was still a chance of a swift strike. Better still, the allied commanders had guessed, wrongly, that Rupert would not force a battle, and had begun to withdraw to Tadcaster, in the hope of blocking any royalist move south-wards. It was only at nine o'clock in the morning that they real-ized the danger, and desperate orders were sent to bring back the advance units. The chance of a quick attack against an unpre-pared enemy was there. But Rupert was vastly outnumbered, and could only fight with the support of Newcastle's infantry in York. It was Newcastle's reluctance to allow his troops, weary after a long siege, to march out for battle, and the delay it caused, that forced Rupert to engage in a conventional battle, on an open field, against a larger enemy army. Defeat was now likely, and it was made certain by Rupert's sudden disappearance from the battlefield soon after the fighting had started.

While Rupert, as the senior general, was ultimately to blame for losing at Marston Moor, there are two others who must share the responsibility. The first is Charles I, whose orders encouraged Rupert to make the rash decision to fight. Second, Newcastle's delay in deploying his troops in support of Rupert robbed the royalists of the chance of a surprise attack, and gave the allies the initiative. Politics and personality meant that Rupert's brilliantly executed campaign ended in a massive defeat.

## Fairfax and the Naseby campaign, June 1645

Sir Thomas Fairfax was unlike Prince Rupert in many ways: a modest man without political ambitions, his approach to soldier-ing was methodical and level-headed. He had learned the art of generalship not in the major battles of the early years of the civil war but in the local arena of his native Yorkshire. In one impor-tant respect, however, Fairfax's position in the early summer of

1645 was the same as that of Rupert a year earlier – his independence as a commander was restricted by his superiors, who
tried to control fast-moving events from afar. In Fairfax's case, the
controllers were the members of the Committee of Both Kingdoms, which had run the war effort in England and Scotland
for the previous eighteen months, and whose members included
the ousted general the earl of Essex and his friends. It was their
instructions that led Fairfax to lead the new field army (the 'New
Model Army') to march first to Taunton in Somerset and then to
Oxfordshire in the spring of 1645, and he was only freed from
their attentions in early June, when he was given orders 'to attend
the motions of the king's army in such way, as being on the place,
you may judge to be the best'.

Political interference aside, Fairfax was faced with another
huge task in the spring of 1645: fashioning the New Model
Army into an efficient fighting force. The army was largely made
up of troops from the armies of the earls of Essex and Manchester
and of Sir William Waller, and these needed to be restructured, in
some cases amalgamated, and made to feel part of a new whole.
Fairfax undertook this task with great energy, insisting on greater
levels of discipline, ensuring regular pay, and, above all, weeding
out suspect officers (especially Scots) and securing the services
of the best men available. This led to immense opposition from
Westminster, again led by those MPs and peers associated with
Essex, but Fairfax mostly got his own way. Crucially, he insisted
on having the popular and experienced Oliver Cromwell as his
lieutenant-general of horse. Fairfax's critics were scornful. As one
of the Scottish commissioners, Robert Baillie, put it, 'this new-
modelled army consists, for the most part, of new, inexperienced
soldiers; few of the officers are thought capable of their places'.
The reality was not so bad. In a short few weeks, the New Model
Army had been moulded in Fairfax's own image. It remained an
unknown quantity, but it was not divided.

The Naseby campaign began with the shock of the royalist
attack on Leicester, which was taken by Rupert on 28 May. It

**Figure 6** Thomas Fairfax. Engraving by Wenceslaus Hollar.

was this that prompted the committee to release Fairfax from interference, and he was soon marching north to see if the king's army could be brought to battle. His progress was painfully slow, but deliberately so. As yet the intentions of the royalist army were unknown, and Fairfax wanted to keep them guessing about his own plans. A slow march also allowed him to gather together as many men as possible, and to arrange for supplies to be brought from a wide radius – which was essential in keeping the army from dispersing over a wide area in search of food and fodder.

On 13 June, Fairfax's scouts located the royalists at Market Harborough, and the New Model Army advanced to the village of Naseby. By this time, Fairfax was aware that the king had not been joined by additional forces under Goring, as had been feared. The royalist scouts had been lax, and the king could not withdraw his forces without risking being attacked as he did so. Instead, he advanced, and the battle took place on the open fields to the north of Naseby on 14 June. This was ground of Fairfax's choosing, and his army was considerably larger than that of the king. The cautious approach had paid off.

Fairfax had won the advantage at Naseby just as surely as Rupert at Marston Moor; but fighting a battle was a very different matter. Fairfax approached the problem coolly. While this was to be a conventional battle, with the foot in the centre and the horse on the wings, Fairfax used the terrain to good effect by withdrawing his main force behind the brow of the hill. This would keep the royalists guessing as to his strength and deployment. He also anchored his left wing on the enclosures known as Sulby Hedges and, apparently at Cromwell's suggestion, he ordered the dragoons under Colonel Okey to hold the hedges, allowing them to rake the advancing royalist cavalry at close range. The right wing was put under the command of Cromwell himself. Fairfax did not join the cavalry. Instead, he stayed with the infantry, moving from regiment to regiment with his head uncovered, so that the men could see their general was facing the same dangers as they did. As a result, he was on hand to commit the cavalry reserves at the crucial point, ensuring the comprehensive defeat of the king's army.

If Marston Moor lost the king the north, Naseby lost him the war. Fairfax's methodical approach to soldiering – recruiting and

**FAIRFAX IN THE FIRING LINE. BULSTRODE WHITELOCKE'S ACCOUNT OF THE BATTLE OF NASEBY, 14 JUNE 1645**

The general had his helmet beat off, and riding in the field bareheaded up and down from one part of his army to another, to see how they stood and what advantage might be gained, and coming up to his own lifeguard commanded by Colonel Charles D'Oyley, he was told by him that he exposed himself to too much danger, and the whole army thereby, riding bareheaded in the fields and so many bullets flying about him, and D'Oyley offered his general his helmet; but he refused it, saying, 'It is well enough, Charles'.

Source: quoted in Glenn Foard, *Naseby: The Decisive Campaign* (Barnsley, Pen and Sword, 2004), 271–2.

reforming the army, concentrating his forces, out-scouting his opponent and forcing battle on his own terms – had ensured that he won the battle as well as the campaign. He may have lacked Rupert's dash, but his personal bravery was unquestionable, and he enjoyed the loyalty of his men. Crucially, he had managed to free himself from the unhelpful advice of his political masters, and he was blessed with subordinates and colleagues who were willing to obey his instructions. Where Rupert had Newcastle, Fairfax had Cromwell.

# Cromwell and the Preston campaign, August 1648

The defeat of the royalists in the first civil war had not led to a peace settlement. Instead, Charles I prevaricated, hoping that the political divisions among the parliamentarians would give him the upper hand. In this, he was only partially right. Despite their differences, the moderates and Presbyterians were not yet ready to become full-blown royalists, and only the Scots, who feared

Parliament's intentions, and wanted to believe the king's promises of religious reform, were prepared to back him.

In the early summer of 1648, the series of uprisings known as the second civil war caused alarm at Westminster, but they were put down with relative ease. The greatest danger came from the Scottish army, led by the 1st duke of Hamilton, which crossed the English border at Carlisle on 8 July. Fairfax was busy besieging the royalists in Colchester, so the campaign against the Scots was conducted by his lieutenant-general, Oliver Cromwell.

Cromwell was an unlikely soldier. A minor country gentleman from Huntingdonshire, he had had no military experience before the summer of 1642, when, at the age of forty-three, he found himself involved in the desperate struggle to prevent the king's friends from taking control of Cambridge and its environs. By the beginning of 1643, Cromwell had become a colonel of horse, and was soon famous for his victories in a number of cavalry actions in the east of England, and for the religious dedication to the cause that he encouraged among his troops. He was also known as a staunch defender of his subordinate officers against the criticism of those who were suspicious of religious fanaticism.

### CROMWELL'S MILITARY PHILOSOPHY. CROMWELL TO THE SUFFOLK COMMITTEE, 29 AUGUST 1643

If you choose godly honest men to be captains of horse, honest men will follow them, and they will be careful to mount such...I had rather have a plain russet-coated captain that knows what he fights for, and loves what he knows, than that which you call a gentleman and is nothing else. I honour a gentleman that is so indeed. I understand Mr Margery hath honest men will follow him; if so, be pleased to make use of him. It much concerns your good to have conscientious men.

Source: Abbott, *Writings and Speeches*, i. 256.

As the lieutenant-general of the Eastern Association, Cromwell played a crucial role in defeating Rupert at Marston Moor, and as Fairfax's number two he was largely responsible for the great parliamentarian victory at Naseby. In 1648, Cromwell was at the height of his powers as a commander, and his popularity in the New Model Army rivalled that of Fairfax himself.

When Hamilton arrived at Carlisle, Cromwell was in South Wales, besieging Pembroke Castle, and the initial problem was how to get his troops north before the Scots could penetrate further south through Lancashire, or cross the Pennines into Yorkshire. The only parliamentarian forces in the north were a small brigade led by John Lambert, who did his best to harass the Scots, while avoiding being overwhelmed in a straight fight. Pembroke fell on 11 July, and Cromwell marched north. After months of campaigning, his troops were tired and poorly equipped, but by sheer force of personality Cromwell maintained discipline and prevented mutiny or desertion.

Like Rupert before Marston Moor, Cromwell had to move fast; but, as with Fairfax before Naseby, he was also aware of the need for careful preparation. The solution was to arrange

### CROMWELL ON THE MARCH. A SOLDIER'S VIEW OF THE PRESTON CAMPAIGN, AUGUST 1648

Our brigade came hither [Leicester] today. Our marches long, and want of shoes and stockings, gives discouragement to our soldiers, having received no pay these many months to buy them, nor can we procure any unless we plunder, which was never heard of by any under the lieutenant-general's conduct, nor will be, though they march barefoot, which many have done since our advance from Wales.

Source: *The Moderate*, quoted by S.R. Gardiner, *The History of the Great Civil War* (4 volumes, Moreton-in-Marsh, Windrush Press, (1987)), iv. 178.

for supplies to be sent ahead of the army, and on 5 August, on his arrival at Nottingham, there were 2,500 pairs of shoes from Northampton and 2,500 pairs of stockings from Coventry waiting for him. Cromwell also needed more men. At Doncaster on 5 August, he was joined by the artillery train from Hull, and in the next few days he replaced new recruits with experienced troops drawn from the siege of Pontefract. On 12 August, he was at Wetherby, where he met Lambert. There was no question of who would take charge of the campaign, as Cromwell had recently secured a commission to command all the parliamentarian troops in the north of England.

While Cromwell was marching north, gathering supplies and more troops, and establishing his authority, Hamilton was slowly moving south through Lancashire, preoccupied with settling the differences between his subordinates. Hamilton was no soldier, and he tended to defer to the more experienced, but prickly, earl of Callander. The best of the troops were the northern royalists under Marmaduke Langdale, who were busy skirmishing with Lambert, and the Scottish regiments brought from Ireland by Robert Monro. Monro and Callander soon fell out, and, rather than imposing his own authority, Hamilton ordered Monro to escort the artillery, which were on the road far behind the main army. The army halted at Preston to allow Langdale and Monro to catch up, and Hamilton, unaware that Cromwell was on the other side of the Pennines, allowed his cavalry to advance to Wigan, fifteen miles south, to search for fodder and supplies. Hamilton's army outnumbered Cromwell's forces by two to one, but they were spread out across Lancashire, and the senior officers were hopelessly divided.

Cromwell saw his chance. Leaving the cumbersome artillery behind him, he marched across the Pennines using the same route as Rupert four years before, and struck at Hamilton's main body at Preston. This was an audacious attack upon a larger enemy, and if it had failed the road south would have been clear for the

**Figure 7** Oliver Cromwell. Portrait by Robert Walker c. 1649.

Scots to reach the royalist heartlands of Wales and the marches. The greatest risk was that Cromwell would be caught in the front by Hamilton and in the rear by Monro. Only a lightning attack would work.

Cromwell's greatest ally was Hamilton himself. Ignorant of the enemy's approach, Hamilton was busy overseeing the march of the Scots infantry over the River Ribble, having left Langdale to guard the rear. It was Langdale's men who bore the brunt of Cromwell's attack on 17 August, and even then Callander persuaded Hamilton not to go to assist Langdale but to continue the crossing in order to regroup on the far side of the river. Langdale had been abandoned to his fate. During the fierce fighting that ensued, Langdale's troops were forced back into Preston, and Lambert outflanked the royalist position and secured the bridge over the Ribble. The next day, the New Model Army foot forced their way across the bridge and defeated the demoralized Scots. The invasion had been defeated, and Cromwell could now march north, to impose a political settlement on the Scottish nation.

At Preston, Cromwell's bold stroke had sliced Hamilton's army in two, and defeated each part in turn. If Rupert had managed a similarly quick strike at Marston Moor, the king might have won the war four years before. In other ways, Cromwell had learned from Fairfax the importance of concentrating forces, keeping the enemy in the dark, and ensuring his troops were well supplied and in good heart. He also enjoyed something that Rupert never had, and that Fairfax had only gained at the very last moment: independence of command. In the midst of the panic that attended the Scottish invasion, Cromwell was able to demand the supplies he needed, and to secure unchallenged authority over the theatre of operations. The case of Cromwell at Preston demonstrates what was necessary for a commander to be successful. Much of this was a matter of basic military competence and an ability to capitalize on the mistakes of one's opponents. There was also the question of judgement – of knowing when to attack and when to be cautious – and of relationships – good subordinates and supportive superiors could make the difference between victory and defeat.

Cromwell appears to have had an intuitive understanding of what was required of a successful general – and he displayed the same outstanding qualities at Dunbar in 1650 and Worcester in 1651 as he had done at Preston. Whether he was the best general of the civil wars is a moot point, but what sets him apart is his ability to perform equally well as a politician as he did as a general. Aristocrats such as the earl of Essex were skilled politicians, but their generalship was, perhaps as a consequence, conservative – even indecisive. A natural general, such as Rupert, did not always make the most subtle of politicians. Cromwell stepped between the two worlds with great assurance. He was attuned to the political implications of his military activities, and realized that political influence made the general's job that much easier.

This can also be seen in his later military career. After Preston, he moved north to put pressure on the Scots not to do any further deals with the king or his friends; he made sure that he had political support, and adequate funding, before he embarked on his campaigns in Ireland and Scotland; and he used the final victory, over Charles II at Worcester, as a springboard to become the most important political and military figure in the commonwealth.

# 7
# Politics

English society in the years before the civil war was marked by its conservatism. But what of the theories that lay behind that consensual arrangement, and how had they been adapted to a king like Charles I, who refused to play by the rules? How did the upheavals of the war years lead to an upsurge of radical ideas during the revolutionary years that followed, as well as influencing the growth of printing and the dark arts of propaganda?

## Political theory in 1642

For contemporaries, the relationship between the sovereign and his people was a matter of tradition, precedent, and religion. They looked back to the 'ancient constitution' that had developed over the centuries and was enshrined in the common law, and thus could act as a legitimate curb on excessive royal power, exercised through the king's prerogatives. This sense of the rights of the subject was reinforced by notions imported from the continent that people had a religious duty to oppose an ungodly or evil king – the so-called Calvinist Resistance theory. Such ideas did not mean that 'the people' were innately hostile to the crown. While all worked well, there was no need to put theories of opposition into practice.

However, the early Stuart kings were developing their own notions that elevated monarchy into something altogether more grandiose. Building on the cult of monarchy fostered by Elizabeth I, James I insisted that his right to rule was not the result of a contract with his subjects, but an inalienable, hereditary right, which trumped any appeal to ancient laws and customs. This was underpinned by a growing theology of kingship – the 'divine right of kings' – which saw monarchs as the representatives of God on Earth, and thus above any human law. James was a canny man, however, who realized that such theories could not be used as a basis for stable government. As he wrote in *Basilikon Doron*, 'a good king will not only delight to rule his subjects by the law, but even will conform himself in his own actions thereunto'. In other words, a sensible king made sure that absolutist tendencies were kept on a tight rein. With both king and subjects exercising restraint, political consensus could be achieved, and conflict avoided.

Charles I, however, refused to allow the monarchy to be limited in this way, and used the theory of 'divine right' to override the 'ancient constitution'. His decision to dispense with Parliament and embark on a period of personal rule had its counterpart in the increasingly formalized court, which made the king inaccessible to all but a small clique of courtiers. The king's distance from his people, and his political intransigence, contributed to the crisis of the late 1630s and the calling of the Long Parliament in November 1640. This parliament saw a concerted attempt by the king's opponents to introduce formal limits to royal power – largely by changing the advisers around the king, rather than by undermining the position of the monarchy itself. By the summer of 1641, it was obvious that such an approach was unlikely to succeed, because the king did not consider himself morally bound by any agreement that compromised his divinely ordained powers.

In reaction, Parliament made faltering steps towards asserting its own claim to exercise power as the representative of the people.

In part, this was inspired by the medieval notion of the 'king's two bodies' – that the private person of the king could be separated from his function as head of state. In an emergency, the latter role could be exercised by the 'high court of parliament', acting on behalf of the people. Some writers, notably Henry Parker, were developing such theories in the summer of 1642, and they had already been overtaken by events: the passing of the militia ordinance in March had already asserted Parliament's right to legislate 'in this time of imminent danger', and the Nineteen Propositions of June was based on similar principles. Even the most radical of parliamentarians were not prepared to pursue such ideas to their logical extension, however. No one questioned Charles I's right to be king, still less raised the possibility of government without the monarchy. Instead, most parliamentarians argued that their actions were part of an honourable tradition, going back to Tudor times and the later Middle Ages, of rebelling to put pressure on the crown, to make an obstinate king change his mind.

In 1642, it was hoped by both parties that peace could be arranged quickly – even before a battle could be fought. Parliament's

## RELUCTANT REBELS: PARLIAMENT'S VOTES TO RAISE AN ARMY, 12 JULY 1642

Resolved, upon the question, that an army shall be forthwith raised for the safety of the king's person, defence of both houses of parliament, and of those who have obeyed their orders and commands, and preserving of the true religion, the laws, liberty and peace of the kingdom.

Resolved, upon the question, that this House doth declare that in the cause...they will live and die with the earl of Essex, whom they have nominated general in this cause.

Resolved, upon the question, that a petition shall be framed, to move his majesty to a good accord with his parliament to prevent a civil war.

Source: Gardiner, *Constitutional Documents*, 261.

votes in the weeks before the conflict broke out announced that their primary aim was to protect the king's best interests (as they saw them) and to persuade him to join with them in preventing war. This was not the whole picture, of course, but it made clear that they considered the aim of the war to be the restoration of the *status quo ante bellum*. The king would have agreed with them. But his idea of what that status quo might look like was very different from Parliament's.

## Factional politics, 1642–7

The first civil war and its immediate aftermath were dominated by military necessity and factional division, rather than by further developments among political theorists. This was a common theme for both sides. As the first shots were fired in 1642, the royalists began to divide into loose groupings, according to what they hoped to achieve. There were some around the king, notably the earl of Dorset and Lord Falkland, who were keen to make peace at the earliest opportunity; but they were opposed by hardliners, including Lord Digby and Prince Rupert, who wanted a total victory and an imposed peace. They were supported by Charles's Catholic queen, Henrietta Maria. Between the two groupings were unhappy figures such as Sir Edward Hyde (later earl of Clarendon) and the marquess of Hertford, who believed that the king should be bounded by the rule of law, that Parliament's rights should be respected, and the Church of England upheld in its traditional form. For them, negotiation from a position of strength would be the best outcome.

As it became clear that the war would not be decided quickly, and as initial peace negotiations at Oxford in the spring of 1643 failed, the hard-liners became dominant. Yet the defeat at Marston Moor in July 1644 caused a split between Lord Digby, who pressed for more Irish or even French troops to be brought over,

> ## THE DILEMMA OF A MODERATE ROYALIST: EXTRACT FROM THE COMMONPLACE BOOK OF SIR JOHN STRANGWAYS, 23 NOVEMBER 1646
>
> …'tis not safe for the state
> To make the sword the judge of this debate.
> If in this war the parliament prevail,
> To us and ours they do the war entail.
> And if the king regains his crown by arms,
> Then we may thank ourselves for all our harms.
> For having so got all into his hands
> He is made lord of all our lives and lands.
> And if we our laws and liberties…have lost.
>
> Source: Beinecke Library, Osborn Shelves b. 304, p. 92, quoted in David L. Smith, *Constitutional Royalism and the Search for Settlement, c.1640–1649* (Cambridge, 1994), 253.

and Rupert, who now thought accommodation with Parliament was the only way to salvage the kingdom. Rupert sought new allies from among the 'doves', including Hertford and the duke of Richmond. As we saw in the last chapter, divisions among the courtiers could cause massive problems on the battlefield, and Marston Moor was followed, in June 1645, by the destruction of the king's army at Naseby, and, a year later, the surrender of Oxford itself. By that time, even devoted servants of the king were having second thoughts about the strategy of total victory, as the lament of Sir John Strangways illustrates.

Ultimately, the chaotic political divisions at Oxford were the fault of the king. Charles was too ready to listen to those, like Digby, who remained at court, leaving the field commanders, including Rupert, without political support. The unpopularity of the Catholic queen, and the distasteful schemes to bring in foreign troops, did nothing to settle the worries of those who saw as much danger in victory as in defeat. Worse was to come.

Once the first civil war had ended, the leading royalists remained divided. Some favoured a properly negotiated peace treaty with Parliament, while others encouraged the king to go through the motions of negotiating, while seeking allies abroad who might come to his rescue. Unhappily, Charles agreed with the latter, and began on the path that led to the Engagement with the Scots in the dying weeks of 1647, and the second civil war in the following spring.

Charles I's refusal to compromise was influenced by divisions among his opponents. These divisions can be dated back to the months after the indecisive battle of Edgehill in October 1642, when the fragile parliamentarian consensus fell apart, leaving a variety of groupings with different views on the conduct of the war. During 1643 and 1644, these groupings coalesced and then dissolved, as the war ebbed and flowed. The failure of Parliament's lord general, the earl of Essex, and his aristocratic colleagues to bring victory led to a crisis at Westminster in the winter of 1644–5, when the grouping centred on Viscount Saye and Oliver St John forced through the Self-Denying Ordinance, which prevented MPs and peers from serving in the army – a measure that removed both Essex and Manchester from their commands. This was followed not only by the raising of a combined field army, the New Model Army, but also by the deepening of factional divisions at Westminster.

From this point, it is appropriate to refer to two main 'parties' in the Commons and Lords, the Independents (as the Saye–St John group was known) and the Presbyterians (associated with the earls of Essex and Manchester, and leading MPs Denzil Holles and Sir Philip Stapilton). Politically, these factions were irreconcilable. The Presbyterians sought to restore Charles to most of his powers, but with suitable parliamentarians holding high office, and thus ensuring that crown policies could be kept under control. They were also keen to conciliate the Scots, as their army was the only force capable of standing up to the New Model Army. The Independents wanted more guarantees. Any settlement would require royal power being devolved to the privy council, dominated by Independents, and, as the king was unlikely to agree to this voluntarily, the prerequisite was total victory by the New Model Army. The Scots were to be sent home as soon as possible, and Scotland cut out of any agreement with the king, or any part in the reconquest of Ireland, for that matter.

The end of the civil war in 1646 heightened tensions between the Presbyterians and Independents, as both tried to impose their own settlement on a reluctant king. Charles, hoping to exploit the divisions among his enemies, played for time. The Newcastle Propositions of July 1646 required the king to agree to a Presbyterian system of church government, to allow Parliament to control the army for ten years and to nominate all officers of state, while a number of key royalists would not be pardoned. These proposals had a distinct Presbyterian flavour, but they were unlikely to succeed, and may even have been designed to fail.

In the new year of 1647, the Presbyterians tried to disband the New Model Army, hoping to ship the remnants to Ireland to fight the rebels there. The army, fearing that they would lose all their arrears of pay, reacted angrily, and by May the troops were close to mutiny. This was an opportunity for the Independents, who had close links with the senior officers, especially Cromwell and his son-in-law, Henry Ireton. In August, the New Model Army entered London, and the Independents returned to Westminster in triumph.

In the days before, Ireton, with the assistance of Saye and other Independent grandees, formulated the Independents' own peace deal with the king, known as the *Heads of the Proposals*. This called for regular parliaments, with Parliament having the right to appoint privy councillors and control the army for ten years; it also provided for a tolerant church, with Anglican forms

**Figure 8**   Westminster from the River. Engraving by Wenceslaus Hollar.

– including bishops – recognized but not made compulsory, and very few active royalists were excluded from pardon. These were the most generous terms that Charles had been presented with, but he again refused to take them seriously. According to one of his advisers, the king's reply was scornful: 'You cannot do it without me! You will fall to ruin if I do not sustain you'.

As Charles's words made apparent, the period of factional politics had not addressed the fundamental problem – what to do with a king who refused to be bound by any human authority, or to limit himself. All the attempts to make peace – from the Oxford treaty to the *Heads of the Proposals* – had merely tinkered with the status quo, even though the king demonstrated time and again that he would not accept any limitations to his power. Parliament could try to control the king's councillors and to elevate the status of Parliament, but, without the king's acceptance of such agencies as binding, there was little that could be done to prevent the return of absolute government. Frustration at this impasse was growing, however, fuelled by religious radicals who saw defeat in the civil war as a judgement on the king.

# Revolutionary politics, 1647–51

The Independent faction, in encouraging the New Model Army to intervene in politics in 1647, had set loose forces they would find very difficult to control. The regiments had begun to organize themselves politically, electing representatives, known as agitators, from the ranks of both officers and men. These agitators made contact with civilian radicals, such as John Wildman and William Walwyn – known as the Levellers – to formulate an alternative agenda for reform, *The Agreement of the People*. This called for the overthrow of the 'ancient constitution' of England, radical reform of the legal system, and a parliament that was truly

---

**THE LIMITS OF REVOLUTION: EXTRACT FROM THE PUTNEY DEBATES, 29 OCTOBER 1647**

Colonel Thomas Rainborough: 'I desired that those that had engaged in it [might be included in the franchise]. For really I think that the poorest he that is in England hath a life to live, as the greatest he; and therefore truly, Sir, I think it's clear that every man that is to live under a government ought first by his own consent to put himself under that government; and I do think that the poorest man in England is not at all bound in a strict sense to that government that he hath not had a voice to put himself under...'

Commissary-General Henry Ireton: 'For my part, I think it is no right at all. I think that no person hath a right to an interest or share in the disposing of the affairs of the kingdom, and in determining or choosing those that shall determine what laws we shall be ruled by here – no person hath a right to this, that hath not a permanent fixed interest in this kingdom [by owning property], and those persons together are properly the represented of this kingdom, and consequently are [also] to make up the representers of this kingdom'.

Source: A.S.P. Woodhouse (ed.), *Puritanism and Liberty, being the army debates (1647–9) from the Clarke Manuscripts, with supplementary documents* (London, J.M. Dent and Sons, 1950), 53–4.

representative of the people, who were the source of all authority. This went far further than many in the army were prepared to go, but the Leveller manifesto also played on suspicions that the Independent 'grandees' and the senior army officers were planning to restore the king on terms advantageous only to themselves, and that the ordinary soldiers' rights were at stake. The result was angry exchanges at the meetings of the army council at Putney in late October and early November, in which radical ideas were slapped down by Ireton, Cromwell, and their allies, who still believed that a negotiated settlement with the king was possible.

The second civil war changed everything. The outbreak of the new conflict revealed that Charles could never be trusted; but the solution was not immediately clear. Could he be forced to abdicate in favour of one of his sons? Was it possible to put a king on trial for treason against his own subjects? Behind such vital questions lay a religious imperative. Charles had been defeated in the first civil war by God's Providence, as much as by the arms of the New Model Army. By restarting the war, Charles had refused to abide by God's judgement on him, and had become 'a man of blood' who must be destroyed. This was far further than most MPs were prepared to go, and their moves to conclude a last-minute deal with the king – along similar lines as before – provoked the army to purge the Commons on 6 December 1648. There remained the small matter of the purged Commons lacking the constitutional power to proceed against the king. This was solved by a resolution of 4 January 1649, which simply asserted the sovereignty of the Commons, as the representative of the people.

The execution of Charles I on 30 January 1649 looks like a neat cut-off point in English history, but, in political and constitutional terms, it was anything but. As we saw in Chapter 4, the statutes vital for creating the new commonwealth were remarkably slow in coming. Political theory was playing catch-up. The poet John Milton justified the execution of the king in his book *Eikonoklastes*, which asked the key question: 'wherefore should we not hope to be governed more happily without a king?' Milton, and the propagandist Marchamont Nedham, were among those constructing republican theories during this period, derived from the writings of ancient Rome, and based on the notions of liberty and civic virtue. They argued that a 'free republic' was not only possible, but also desirable.

In the main, however, the new regime tried to justify itself in terms of necessity and the need for stability, rather than presenting carefully considered theories of republican government. Thus, the new oath of support for the commonwealth, the Engagement, formulated in 1649 and imposed across the whole country from January 1650, was in effect an acknowledgement of the de facto legitimacy of the new commonwealth, which was justified as the means 'for the better uniting of this nation'. This foot-dragging was not just a reaction to breaking the taboo of monarchy: it also reflected a tension within the new regime, between the Rump Parliament MPs, who were mostly a conservative bunch, and the radicals within the army, who expected a far-reaching programme akin to *The Agreement of the People*.

This was a time of great excitement and bitter disappointment among the radicals. The Levellers, unhappy with the Rump Parliament's inactivity, fomented mutiny within the army. The Diggers, or 'True Levellers', with their mystical brand of communism, began to till common land in Surrey (and were duly evicted), and in 1651 their leading writer, Gerrard Winstanley, produced his own constitution, *The Law of Freedom in a Platform*, which advocated the redistribution of the land to self-governing communities, as a means of fulfilling God's plan for England. In the same year, the pro-royalist Thomas Hobbes published *Leviathan*, which described a somewhat dystopian vision of government by an absolute monarch, to whom the subjects would surrender their rights in return for protection. Hobbes's view of human nature was grim. He saw life as 'mean, nasty, short and brutish' and reduced human society to 'a war of every man with every man'.

The theories of Winstanley and Hobbes would have little direct impact on politics, but the spirit of radicalism remained alive within the army, and this was bound to cause tensions with its paymasters in Parliament. As yet the crisis was postponed, as the military was preoccupied with the invasion of Ireland and then Scotland. But the stream of providential victories against the Irish and the Scots strengthened the hand of the army and its allies, who saw political theories and constitutional niceties as attempts to limit the will of God.

With the return of Cromwell to Westminster in September 1651, the constitutional question was still open. Cromwell, as lord general, would dissolve the Rump parliament in April 1653, much to the anger of the republicans. An attempt to rule through an assembly of the 'saints' – the Nominated Assembly or Barebone's Parliament – proved unstable, and in December 1653 Cromwell took on a quasi-monarchical role, as lord protector, bound by a written constitution. Ironically, the revolution had ultimately brought the limited monarchy the parliamentarians had sought since 1642, but with a commoner in charge, backed by a standing army and with toleration to religious radicals.

# Print, propaganda, and popular politics

One of the most important political developments during the civil war years was the massive expansion of the production and circulation of printed works, the so-called 'print revolution'. The calling of the Long Parliament in 1640, and the attack on the authority of the crown that followed, coincided with a collapse in the censorship system that had operated in the pre-war years, aided and abetted by the abolition of such bodies as the court of Star Chamber and the court of High Commission.

In particular, there was a sudden explosion in newsbooks. These newsbooks were small pamphlets, usually of eight pages, published weekly and in serial form. The first, entitled *The Heads of Several Proceedings in this Present Parliament*, was published in November 1641, and in a matter of weeks seven other titles had appeared. Over the next decade, there were dozens of different newsbooks, some lasting only a few weeks, others becoming the essential reading matter of the literate public over many months and even years. These naturally became the weapon of choice for politicians. Royalist publications such as *Mercurius Aulicus* locked horns with London-based newsbooks including *Mercurius Britanicus* in a conflict that saw the denigration of the quality of the information provided by rivals, and even *ad hominem* attacks on their editors.

Newsbooks and other publications also became the propaganda tools of factions at Westminster. The Independents gradually took control of the print licensing system during the later 1640s, to the detriment of their Presbyterian opponents and the Scots. Even in defeat the royalists could land savage blows on the parliamentarians through unlicensed pamphlets produced on underground presses.

However, attempts to use the media could sometimes backfire. The trial of Charles I in 1649 was held in public, and the government, unable to keep the details secret, chose instead to manage how that information was disseminated through the employment of two experienced editors, Henry Walker and Gilbert Mabbott. These men used their various newsbooks to produce a near-daily account of proceedings, with a pro-government gloss. Unfortunately, the king's decision not to enter a plea, and his haughty disdain of the court, could not be suppressed, and instead of inspiring support for the regicide these pro-parliamentarian newsbooks became a key source for royalists, who drew comfort from their accounts of the king's bravery and used them to create their own publications praising the royal martyr.

As the case of the reporting of the king's trial demonstrates, those producing printed works had to surrender them to the readership, who might interpret them in all sorts of unexpected ways. There is no doubt that the appetite for print was there, or that it increased during the 1640s. Although most pamphlets and newsbooks had a relatively small print run, perhaps in the hundreds, there is evidence that the more popular titles ran to several thousand copies. Each of these would be read by many people, and read out to still more, allowing even the illiterate to engage in political debate.

Although levels of literacy were low, with perhaps a third of men and a tenth of women being able to read and write, there were great variations between rural and urban areas, different regions and social classes. In London, literacy was high, and Nehemiah Wallington, a wood-turner, recorded in his many notebooks his passion for reading – even to the detriment of his business. More importantly, Wallington and his friends used the information in the newsbooks and other printed sources to come to their own conclusions about what was happening in the country.

Other ordinary people embraced print as a ready way to influence opinion, from the pro-episcopal petitioners of 1641 to the radical visionary Gerrard Winstanley in 1649. Although 'public opinion' as such probably did not exist in its modern form, there is no doubt that many individuals across England were encouraged to engage with politics through the medium of print.

The details of readership and reception remain obscure, however. In only a very few cases can the way in which texts were read be stated with any certainty, as the cultural nuances are mostly lost to us. Street ballads provide a fascinating example. These were printed on single, large sheets, and sold by the thousand to private individuals or to those such as innkeepers who posted them up publicly. Many have overt political themes, but we should take care

## POPULAR REACTIONS: EXTRACT FROM 'THE WORLD IS TURNED UPSIDE DOWN' (1646)

To conclude, I'll tell you news that's right
Christmas was killed at Naseby Fight.
Charity was slain at that same time,
Jack Tell Truth too, a friend of mine,
Likewise then did die;
Roast beef and shred pie,
Pig, goose and capon no quarter found.
Yet let's be content, and the time lament,
You see the world is quite turned round.

Source: Christopher Marsh, *Music and Society in Early Modern England* (Cambridge, Cambridge UP, 2010), 305.

not to be too literal when considering them. The refrain 'the clean contrary way' may signal that the words are ironic in nature. The tunes specified may give other clues. Thus, 'The World is Turned Upside Down', a sombre account of measures taken by Parliament against popular pastimes and entertainments published in 1646, was set to the upbeat, and famously royalist, tune 'The King Enjoys his Own Again'. What had been a depressing catalogue becomes, through association, a song that is both reassuring and uplifting. In civil war politics, things are not always what they seem.

# 8

# Religion

## Royalist religion

There is no doubt that at the beginning of the civil war England was deeply divided on religious lines. In the 1630s, the rise of the high church 'Laudians', who emphasized the sacraments and ceremonial in services, had provoked a reaction among the 'puritans', who wished to remodel the church to bring it closer to the Calvinist Church of Geneva. The political crisis of 1640–1 was fuelled by the desire of many to reverse the unpopular Laudian reforms, but the 'root and branch' changes advocated by the parliamentarian leadership in 1641–2 alienated many people who were deeply attached to the traditional Church of England, and they provided strong support for the king when hostilities broke out in the summer of 1642. The king's party in 1642 was not therefore the Laudians in arms – quite the opposite. Most royalists wanted a return to the church as it had been under Elizabeth I and James I, with bishops and the Book of Common Prayer, and undergirded by a theology that sought the middle way – the *via media* – between Geneva and Rome.

Charles was quick to respond to this by distancing himself from the unpopular Laudians in the early years of the war. Archbishop Laud was allowed to languish in the Tower (and there was no attempt to prevent his execution in 1645), while more moderate bishops were brought back into royal councils, including enemies of Laud, such as John Williams (of Lincoln and then York) and James Ussher (of Armagh). Charles also proclaimed his intention of upholding 'the established and true reformed Protestant religion as it stood in its beauty in the happy days of Queen Elizabeth, without any connivance of popery'.

The new emphasis on tradition and conservatism did not last long, however. There were still Laudian sympathizers at court, and from the mid-1640s Laud's protégés, especially William Juxon, bishop of London, and staunch defenders of episcopacy and critics of Calvinism, such as Jeremy Taylor and Henry Hammond, were important figures around the king. These Laudians vied for influence with a powerful Roman Catholic clique at Oxford (encouraged by Charles's French queen, Henrietta Maria), but at the end of the first civil war, as at the beginning, the vast majority of the king's supporters should be classed as 'Prayerbook Protestants'.

The defeat of the king in 1646 made the Anglican position very vulnerable. Parliament had already embarked on wide-ranging reforms, and the structures of the church were slowly being dismantled. This was a drawn-out process: there had been moves to purge the church of ceremonies and vestments, choirs and organs in 1643–4; Christmas and other religious festivals were outlawed in 1644; the Prayer Book had been formally banned in 1645; and bishops were finally abolished in the autumn of 1646.

In the years that followed, any hopes that a lasting political settlement might bring a return to the old church structures faded still further, as the king made it clear that he was prepared to accept a modified (and greatly weakened) episcopacy. This was accepted by some of the king's clerical advisers, who explored the possibility of agreeing to toleration for the sects in return for guarantees of the survival of the Anglican Church. Others saw this compromise – or, worse still, the acceptance of Presbyterianism for a limited period – as a betrayal. A church settlement was as elusive as a political agreement, however.

Instead, the survival of Anglicanism from the later 1640s until the Restoration depended on three factors. The first was the continuing loyalty of many ordinary people to the old forms, which led to widespread refusal to accept Parliament's reforms, and allowed an underground church community to flourish. Influential clergymen were welcomed to the houses of the royalist gentry, and ministered in private chapels to worshippers from the household and beyond; festivals such as Christmas and Easter were celebrated behind closed doors. Some were more brazen. There were complaints from Dorset and Essex in the winter of 1647–8 that the Prayer Book was being used openly in many churches. Later, modified versions of the Prayer Book were produced by clerics such as Jeremy Taylor and Robert Sanderson, to get round the ban on the old liturgy. The second factor was the decision by the New Model Army and its allies to bring the king to public trial and to execute him in January 1649. Charles's dignity did much to revive loyalty to the monarchy, and his self-presentation as a martyr for the church inspired Anglicans to continue steadfast in the faith. The 'king's book', the *Eikon Basilike*, published soon afterwards, reinforced this image of Charles, and helped to establish a powerful emotional attachment to the monarchy among the defeated royalists. The third factor was the failure of the parliamentarians to agree a new church settlement, or to implement it effectively.

## Parliament, Protestant churches, and sects

During the first civil war, the general assumption in parliamentary circles was that any new church settlement would be along Presbyterian lines. The essential element of this was a strict hierarchy. The bottom tier was formed by the parishes, each with elected 'elders', including the minister, who supervised the moral and religious behaviour of their people. The parishes were in turn overseen by the classes, which chose ministers and elders, and the classes reported to a synod or assembly, which governed the church. For the more extreme (or 'rigid') Presbyterians, the best model for England was the Scottish Kirk, which had operated a system that came very close to the ideal established in Geneva by John Calvin a century before.

In order to establish a Presbyterian system of their own, in 1643, Parliament created the Westminster Assembly, made up of ministers and politicians, to advise on various aspects of doctrine and government. One of the principal fruits of this was the replacement of the Prayer Book by the Directory of Public Worship,

## PRESBYTERIAN FORMS: EXTRACTS FROM THE DIRECTORY OF PUBLIC WORSHIP, 1645

Reading of the Word in the congregation, being part of the public worship of God (wherein we acknowledge our dependence upon him, and subjection to him) and one means sanctified by Him for the edifying of His people, is to be performed by the pastors and teachers.

Preaching of the Word, being the power of God unto salvation, and one of the greatest and most excellent works belonging to the ministry of the Gospel, should be so performed that the workman need not be ashamed but may save himself, and those that hear him.

[At Communion,] the table being before decently covered, and so conveniently placed that the communicants may orderly sit about it, or at it, the minister is to begin the action with sanctifying and blessing the elements of bread and wine set before him...

[On Sunday,] what time is vacant, between or after the solemn meetings of the congregation in public, be spent in reading, meditation, repetition of sermons; especially by calling their families to an account of what they have heard, and catechising of them... singing of psalms, visiting the sick, relieving the poor and such like duties of piety, charity and mercy, accounting the Sabbath a delight.

which was authorized in 1645. The Directory was made up of guidelines for worship, rather than fixed forms and set prayers, and put a suitably Calvinist emphasis on Bible reading, preaching, and the observation of Sundays as the Christian Sabbath. The key player in all this was the properly trained and ordained minister, who was to lead the parish as a father led his family.

The rigidity of the Presbyterian system was troubling for many of the former puritans who had been used to a much looser arrangement, with individual congregations taking care of themselves, and individual Christians making their own decisions based on conscience, guided by the Bible and personal prayer. Within such congregations commitment was very high, and the members saw themselves as 'visible saints'. The movement was especially strong in the parliamentarian heartlands of East Anglia and Lincolnshire, and was also important in the New Model Army regiments. Theologically, these 'Independents' were almost identical to their Presbyterian cousins, but they were violently opposed to the set forms offered by the Scottish system. Their objections became focused on the single issue of 'liberty of conscience' – the demand that congregations could opt out of a formal national church. This made a mockery of the strict Presbyterian system, and was also seen as a threat because it allowed individuals to interpret the Bible – and even preach – without being ordained.

The result of this disagreement was seen in 1647, when the Presbyterians were challenged by the Independents supported by the New Model Army, and the result was a watering down of the plans for church government. Only a minority of English counties had even the semblance of a Presbyterian church system by the end of the decade, and only in London and Lancashire were classes fully developed. Nor were congregations usually independent, instead coming under the influence of lay patrons or local politicians. A truly 'national' church, uniform in worship and theology, remained unattainable throughout the different regimes of the 1650s.

This split between the Presbyterians and the Independents was important in encouraging the survival of Anglicanism. The impotence of the parliamentarians to root out the old church can be seen in an ordinance of August 1647 against those ministers 'put out of their livings by authority of parliament', who 'by force or other ways have entered upon the churches and gained possession of the parsonages, tithes and profits', with the connivance of the local congregations.

This was not the only problem that was apparent in the late 1640s. While the main denominations wrangled, other groups prospered. Chief among them were the Baptist churches. As yet, the Baptists were not a coherent whole, rather a series of interconnected meetings, some growing out of existing Independent congregations. What united them was a belief in adult Baptism, which was part of a public avowal of faith, and they strongly rejected the notion, prevalent in other churches, that Baptism was a rite, performed by a minister, which initiated small babies into the church. The Baptists saw this process of conversion and proclamation and Baptism as entirely voluntary, and, like the Independents, they were intensely congregational and suspicious of any national church structure. Many of them were also convinced that the breakdown of the monarchy and the civil wars were a sign of the last days – the millennium, when Christ would come again to rule over the saints.

The millenarian views of the Baptists were echoed by a number of radical sects. They were small in numbers but their effect on the mainstream churches was disproportionate, as their views were alarming. The Seekers, associated with the Welsh preacher William Erbery, saw themselves as saints awaiting the millennium, but they also questioned the divinity of Christ and believed that all men could be saved. The Ranters – who may not have existed as a distinct group at all – rejected both moral and religious law and denied the Last Judgement, claiming that the saints could not sin. According to the author of *A Single Eye*, published in

1649: 'swearing, drunkenness, adultery and theft were not sinful unless the person guilty of them apprehended them to be so'. Such ideas were deeply shocking in such a conservative society. Another group was the Diggers, or True Levellers, led by the mystic Gerrard Winstanley. The Diggers broke the social norms by cultivating common ground and arguing for equality among people based on the 'inner light' shining in each believer. This idea of an inner light was shared by many other groups, and was common among Independents and Baptists, but is most famously associated with the Quakers, who emerged at the very end of the civil wars under the guidance of George Fox. Another millenarian sect was the Fifth Monarchists, who believed the millennium (and the 'fifth monarchy', that of Christ) was imminent, and who were intent on pursuing their radical agenda politically. Again, this was a group that found support in the army, encouraged by Colonel Thomas Harrison.

Another group of parliamentarians needs to be considered: those who do not easily fit into any of the above categories. Among them could be included the dour Cornish MP Francis Rous, a friend of Scottish divines and a member of the Presbyterian Westminster Assembly, who could also write in favour of liberty of conscience. Or Richard Baxter, who did so much to try to bring together the Independent churches into 'associations' and to make common cause with moderate Presbyterians, but whose 'Arminian' theological views made him suspect in the eyes of the more rigid Presbyterians. Or Oliver Cromwell, who is not known to have attended any particular congregation, but for whom the army may have been a kind of 'gathered church'. Cromwell was the great proponent of liberty of conscience, and had several friendly meetings with the Quaker George Fox in later years; but there were definite limits, at least publicly, and he was most comfortable with a church made up only of Presbyterians, Independents, and Baptists. And we must also consider those who travelled through various denominations in search of truth.

Francis Freeman, a New Model Army captain accused in 1650 of having been 'a papist, Protestant, Presbyterian, Antinomian, Independent, Anabaptist, Seeker, etc', retorted by saying that 'I gave God thanks, I had passed through them all'.

## Popular and unpopular religion

A survey of the different religious denominations, and their often fraught interactions, takes us only so far when it comes to understanding the mindset of people during the English Civil War. We know what they were *supposed* to believe, and we often know what they *said* they believed, and from their actions it can sometimes be surmised what they believed in their hearts. Just as the conformist supporters of the Prayer Book can be difficult to detect in contemporary sources, so the general, shared culture of belief is elusive. But these common assumptions, held by almost everyone in England in the mid-seventeenth century, regardless of their social status or their adherence to any particular church, are of great importance to understanding the period.

In the first place, there was a basic belief in universal order: that the world was created by a God who had arranged everything into a series of hierarchies, all ultimately derived from him. In the kingdom, the king was set above the nobility and the gentry, with the lower orders each occupying their allotted position on the ladder until the very bottom rungs, which were occupied by the landless labourers and beggars. The church formed part of this system, and, apart from the more extreme sects, each church tended to acquire a hierarchy over time. Similarly, each village and town had its own hierarchy, as did each family. Indeed, the family was the bedrock of seventeenth-century thinking, with the father, as head of the household, having considerable power over the lesser members – wife, children, and servants. This sense of order was used by royalists, who saw the king (and bishops) as essential to this system, with the monarchy ruling by 'divine right', while the parliamentarians were rebels against God as well as the king. But the royalists did not have a monopoly on order. For much of the civil wars, Parliament sought to restore the king, albeit with safeguards, and the Presbyterian church system was as rigid as the episcopal one.

This belief in a divinely ordained order was closely connected to the idea of divine Providence – the belief that God intervened in human affairs, guiding not only the great affairs of state but also the everyday lives of individuals. The careful observation and analysis of these signs of divine approval or displeasure was a constant preoccupation among royalists and parliamentarians alike, even if it was most closely associated with radical religion. When the leading parliamentarian Lord Brooke was killed at the siege of Lichfield in 1643, the royalist press saw his end as a punishment for provoking the Almighty.

### A ROYALIST REACTION TO THE DEATH OF LORD BROOKE, WHILE BESIEGING LICHFIELD CATHEDRAL, MARCH 1643

It was...observed (besides his being killed on St Chad's Day, by whose name, as being the first bishop of the Mercians that the church which he assaulted is, and hath anciently been, called) that he who had so often vaunted that he hoped to see the day when one stone of St Paul's in London should not be left one upon another, should be killed in the eye, and the lid not touched. That he who did dislike the Litany for no one thing more than for the prayer therein 'against sudden death' should be killed stone dead (the bullet passing through the eye unto the throat) and not speak one word. Which passages and observations I wish were heartily considered of by his accomplices, who being as deep as he is in this rebellion against God and the king, have little reason to expect any better ends, if they have not worse.

Source: *Mercurius Aulicus*, 11th week (18 March 1643), pp. 133–4.

**PROVIDENCE: OLIVER CROMWELL TO SPEAKER
LENTHALL, 20 AUGUST 1648, AFTER HIS VICTORY
OVER THE SCOTS AT PRESTON**

Surely, Sir, this is nothing but the hand of God, and wherever anything in this world is exalted, or exalts itself, God will pull it down, for this is the day wherein He alone will be exalted. It is not fit for me to give advice, nor to say a word what use should be made of this, more than to pray you, and all that acknowledge God, that they would exalt Him, and not hate His people, who are as the apple of His eye, and for whom even kings shall be reproved. And that you would take courage to do the work of the Lord in fulfilling the end of your magistracy, in seeking the peace and welfare of the people of this land, that all that will live quietly and peaceably may have countenance from you, and they that are implacable and will not leave troubling the land may speedily be destroyed out of the land. And if you take courage in this, God will bless you, and good men will stand by you, and God will have glory, and the land will have happiness by you in despite of all your enemies.

Source: Abbott, *Writings and Speeches*, i. 638.

One of the greatest exponents of these 'divine dispensations' was Oliver Cromwell, and his interpretation of the New Model Army's victory against the king in the second civil war as a sign of divine anger against 'this man of blood' would have a direct impact on the regicide.

Providentialism also made a deep impression on ordinary people. London wood-turner Nehemiah Wallington filled note-book after notebook with fearful accounts of public and private events, and his speculations as to what they could mean. *The Soldier's Pocket Bible*, a short digest of biblical passages published in London in 1643, emphasized obedience ('A soldier must not do wickedly', 'a soldier must not fear his enemies'), but also provided reassurance that God was in control ('though God's people have the worst, yet it cometh of the Lord', 'let soldiers know, and all of us know, that if we obtain any victory over our enemies, it is our duty to give all the glory to the Lord'). In its most extreme form, providentialism shaded into millenarianism. Again, the basic beliefs behind this were commonly held, as God had created the world, and he would bring that world to an end. The question was: how soon?

The sense that God was in control was immensely comforting in a world of otherwise inexplicable natural disasters, diseases, and sudden death – the more so when the civil war threatened to turn the world upside down. Yet the flipside of divine guidance for the believer was his righteous retribution against the unrepentant sinner, which would lead to the everlasting flames of Hell. Damnation and Hell lay at the root of early modern religion. And as real as Hell in the minds of the Christian was the person of the devil himself. The devil's acolytes could be detected even at the highest levels. At different times, both Archbishop Laud and Oliver Cromwell were depicted in the woodcut illustrations of newsbooks as devils in disguise. Prince Rupert was seen as a warlock, protected from injury by the devil and accompanied at all times by his familiar, his dog, Boy. These, and other tales, were reported to Parliament as fact.

Much of this was routine insult, but beneath it lay genuine anxiety, and it was no coincidence that the civil wars also saw an

## WITCHCRAFT. A REPORT TO THE HOUSE OF COMMONS, 25 SEPTEMBER 1643

It is reported that a witch of Prince Rupert's army came over the river, being very deep, without being wet; and being suspected for a spy, was shot at by one of the parliament soldiers in the breast, which hurt her not, only it made a black spot on her breast. After, a soldier thrust at her in the poll [head] with the butt end of his musket and killed her. After she was dead, they shot two bullets at her breast naked, and could not pierce her.

Source: Walter Yonge's diary, BL, Additional MS 18778, f. 55v.

upsurge of cases involving the devil's favourite disciples: witches. In the most famous incident, for two years from 1645, Matthew Hopkins, the 'witchfinder general', ranged around East Anglia examining suspected witches and encouraging neighbours to denounce one another, leading to an epidemic of misery across the region. The close connection between the witch craze and the stress of war is suggested by the report of witch trials in Suffolk in one parliamentarian newsbook in the summer of 1645: 'Some of them confessed they had been in the king's army, and have sent out some of their hags to serve them…his majesty's army it seems is beholding to the devil; you may be sure it is a just cause where the devil takes part'.

The other great bugbear of this period was the Roman Catholic Church. For the vast majority, the pope was the Antichrist foretold in the Book of Revelation, and Catholics were fifth columnists seeking to destroy the Protestant Church and to subject England to foreign tyranny. In August 1642, in the days before the outbreak of civil war, one Catholic priest, Hugh Green, was executed in Dorchester. The crowd, brought up to hate Catholics, and fearful of what the recent rebellion in Ireland might mean for England, reacted with appalling savagery, mutilating the executed corpse and playing football with the head. Their social superiors were not much better. Sir Thomas Trenchard's chaplain had shouted down the priest as he defended himself on the gallows, crying, 'He blasphemeth! Stop the mouth of the blasphemer!', while the sheriff of Dorset did nothing to prevent the crowd running amok once the sentence had been carried out. It was the same mixture of fear and outrage that made the routine execution of Irish Catholic soldiers acceptable during the first civil war, and contributed to the massacres at Basing House in 1645 and Drogheda in 1649. Again, this was a deep-seated prejudice that was shared by many royalists (despite the king's army containing many Catholics from the north-west) as well as by the godly parliamentarians. It was all too easy for the parliamentarian press to play on these fears by making the king and his adherents agents of Rome or of the devil – just as the royalist newsbooks attacked the parliamentarians as rebels and extremists, who were intent on destroying the divinely ordained world order. For both sides, victory and defeat were part of a fundamental struggle between good and evil.

# 9

# War and society

In February 1644, King Charles received a petition by John Oker, the organist of Gloucester Cathedral. In it, Oker recounted 'that about a year and a half since, the petitioner was imprisoned at Gloucester for showing himself loyal to your majesty; and having escaped out of prison, listed himself in your majesty's army under the command of Colonel Windham, where he has been in service almost a year; and after his departure from Gloucester he was plundered and spoiled of all his estate, to the ruin of himself, his wife and children'. Destitute, Oker now turned to the king, asking that he might 'signify your royal pleasure to the dean and chapter of Wells (where he was born and educated) for his admission to the place of a vicar choral of the cathedral church of Wells, there being a vicar's place now lately void by death'. A note on the petition indicates that the request was granted, and Oker was duly recommended to the clergy at Wells. This document (which survives in the Carew papers at the National Archives, PRO 30/5/6, p. 334) provides a vivid example of how civilians were caught up in the civil wars. Oker had been a musician, and was keen to become one again, even if it meant giving up his prestigious job as organist at Gloucester to become a 'vicar choral' (or choir man) at Wells. He was unfortunate to have been a royalist in a parliamentarian city, suffering imprisonment and, on his escape, the ransacking of his house and goods. His family was left destitute, and Oker had no choice but to join the royalist army as an ordinary soldier – a life that was particularly hard for a gentleman to endure.

As Oker's case demonstrates, the world of the civilian and the military often overlapped, with many soldiers being reluctant recruits, anxious to return to civilian life as soon as possible. Certainly, armies were fashioned from such unlikely material. But what of the other side of the coin: the plight of civilians caught up in the civil wars? What was the level of death and destruction, how much damage was done to the fabric of society, and how did people of all social backgrounds cope with the demands of the war years?

# Destruction and disease

It has been calculated that at least 150 towns and 100 villages experienced some form of destruction as a direct consequence of the English Civil War, and to this can be added as many as 200 country houses and castles. The imbalance between urban and rural areas is interesting, and reinforces the impression that the place not to live during the conflict was a town, especially an important one. Small towns often lacked walls and could not easily be defended, and as a result they were not usually useful as permanent bases; the small number of villages that suffered damage testifies to the rather different experience of the war in the countryside. Regional variations could also be marked, as some parts of the country suffered far more than others, especially if they were territory disputed between the two sides for years. The midlands, for example, were fought over incessantly throughout the first civil war, and suffered badly as a result, but in other areas the conflict was localized and brief. The north of England saw little fighting after the parliamentarian victory at Marston Moor in July 1644; Essex and Kent experienced little military activity until the second civil war in 1648; and London was untouched.

Few garrison towns or cities experienced a full-blown siege, and fewer still were stormed by the enemy, but the effects of such an attack could be devastating to the civilian population. Leicester was twice cursed. It was only weakly defended when Prince Rupert's forces arrived before it in 1645, although the houses of the suburbs had been destroyed by the defenders to provide clear fields of fire. The royalists assaulted the town and sacked it, before marching off to defeat at Naseby. The New Model Army then recaptured the town, and it was plundered again, by both the advancing attackers and the retreating defenders, leaving 120 houses destroyed and other property badly damaged. At Gloucester, which underwent a prolonged siege in 1643, most of the destruction was caused by the defenders, as 241 houses in the suburbs were razed, orchards and gardens were destroyed, and meadowland flooded to deny cover to the enemy. The total cost of this was more than £28,000, not including the church of St Owen's, which was demolished by the garrison as it lay immediately outside the city walls. Possibly the worst affected of the English cities was Worcester, which hosted the last stand of Charles Stuart and his Scottish army in the summer of 1651. The battle was mostly fought outside the walls, but the victorious parliamentarians pursued their foes into the city and there began an orgy of destruction that caused lasting damage. The city corporation did not meet for a year, and only intermittently for months after that; £500 was paid by the county to the city for poor relief in 1652; and the revenues of the city were depressed through the 1650s.

The destruction of property was not usually matched by the deliberate killing of non-combatants, but on occasion atrocities happened. In May 1644, the royalist attack on the Lancashire town of Bolton, known as 'the Geneva of the north' for its Puritanism, quickly degenerated into uncontrolled savagery, with unarmed men and women among the dead. Parliament got its revenge in October 1645, when Basing House, a notorious Catholic stronghold in Hampshire, was stormed. The New Model Army soldiers, encouraged by their officers, despatched any who resisted, and killed six Catholic priests in cold blood. What these incidents share is a religious dimension, which brought out the worst in seventeenth-century Englishmen, as they were to demonstrate again in Ireland after 1649.

In England, the number of civilians who died at the hands of soldiers, whether in the midst of conflict or in episodes of casual violence, was relatively small compared with those who died of another unpleasant by-product of early modern warfare: disease. A besieged town was a dangerous place to be, as large numbers of soldiers, some carrying disease and all requiring food, were billeted in civilian houses. The citizens of the royalist garrison of Newark in Nottinghamshire suffered horribly from typhus and plague brought into the town by soldiers.

## DISEASE IN A GARRISON TOWN: THE EXAMPLE OF NEWARK, NOTTINGHAMSHIRE

Newark, situated where the Great North Road crossed the River Trent, was one of the most important royalist towns, and was heavily garrisoned from 1642 until the very end of the first civil war, in May 1646, withstanding many months of blockade and several sieges. A population of perhaps 2,000 people at the beginning of the war was doubled, and at times even trebled, by soldiers and refugees. In these conditions, diseases flourished. One of the most dangerous was typhus – a disease transmitted by human lice – which was endemic in all armies in the early modern period. In Newark, typhus broke out with increasing intensity every winter of the war, and accounted for a significant minority of all deaths between 1643 and 1646, with the peaks of mortality closely correlating with increased military activity in the town. Overall, 12–15% of the inhabitants died from typhus in this period.

> The other main disease was the plague – in this case, the bubonic variety, spread by fleas carried by black rats. The plague arrived in Newark only in the autumn of 1645, and may have been brought to the town by the royalist troops who fled there as other garrisons fell to Parliament, notably Bristol. During the spring of 1646, the number of cases increased, before reaching their height in the summer, and again around 15% of the population perished.
>
> For Newark, typhus was an immediate, and pernicious, result of military occupation, while plague was its short-lived, and extremely unpleasant, legacy.
>
> Source: Stuart B. Jennings, *'These Uncertaine Tymes': Newark and the Civilian Experience of the Civil Wars, 1640–1660* (Nottingham C.C., 2009).

A similar picture emerges from the parish register of Banbury in Oxfordshire, which recorded a threefold increase in deaths among the population as a result of plague between 1643 and 1645, while Plymouth in Devon lost nearly 3,000 people from disease during its long siege. Rural areas – especially those in the hinterland of garrison towns – also experienced high levels of mortality from epidemic diseases. It has been calculated that two and a half times more Devonians died of disease than of violence during the first civil war. The effect on a small community could be devastating. The small village of Caversham in Oxfordshire, just across the Thames from Reading, was garrisoned by parliamentarian troops in the spring and summer of 1643, and the parish registers show the result, as in a nine-week period from the middle of June the number of burials increased six-fold, with some families losing as many as four members in a matter of days.

## Economy

Even when spared the worst effects of the war, the experience of the ordinary civilian was not a happy one. Unpaid soldiers resorted to 'free quarter' in the homes they occupied. The demands for cavalry mounts and cart horses could strip farmers of their main source of motive power – and fertilizer. Sir Samuel Luke, the commander of Newport Pagnell, wrote of the surrounding countryside in November 1644 that 'they have no horses to plough and sow the land'. In pastoral areas, cattle and sheep were easily driven away. Valuable timber was cut down as firewood. Accidents and carelessness could cause as much damage as acts of deliberate destruction. The devastation that could result from a small town

## PLUNDER AND WANTON DESTRUCTION: THE CASE OF DUNBAR, EAST LOTHIAN

The strategic importance of the small port of Dunbar, situated on the Forth Estuary on the road from Berwick-on-Tweed to Edinburgh, was demonstrated in the summer and autumn of 1650, when Cromwell used it as his base during the Scottish campaign. It was on the hills above the town that Cromwell inflicted his crushing defeat on the Scottish army on 3 September. Although Dunbar was not directly involved in the fighting, some of the English soldiers were able to slip away from the battle and relieve the inhabitants of money and goods. This was nothing compared with the wholesale plunder and ruin brought by successive regiments in the following months, as they stopped at Dunbar on their way north to Edinburgh. The total losses of the inhabitants in little more than a year were later calculated to be £115,770, 12s 4d Scots.

A few examples from the 180 or so claims serve to put that figure in more human terms. One burgess, William Purves, lost deal boards and timber, burned by the soldiers for firewood; he had the contents of his bake house destroyed, and also claimed for the burning down of his barn. William Wallance, a farmer, claimed for beer, oats, peas, salt, coal, three carts, two harrows, and a plough, all stolen by the troops. George Thomson, the master of Dunbar grammar school, lost over £300 of goods from his house, as well as his books, money, and 'wearing clothes'. The church was broken into, the poor box emptied, the silverware stolen, and even the velvet 'mort cloths' (draped over coffins) had gone. In short, the soldiers had stripped Dunbar of everything of value. And this was done not in the heat of battle, but on the march, as a matter of course.

Source: National Archives of Scotland, B/18/39 (Dunbar account, c.1651).

acting as a transit camp for soldiers on the march can be seen in the case of Dunbar in Scotland.

Even in less extreme cases, soldiers could act amorally. This disregard for social norms set in very early. In August 1642, when the London regiments marched through Acton in Middlesex on their way to the battle of Edgehill, Serjeant Nehemiah Wharton witnessed an old man, who had been comprehensively robbed, 'sitting on his only stool, with tears flowing down his hoary beard'.

Official exactions could also be hard to bear. Both sides in the first civil war established elaborate systems of taxation, with county collectors supervising a hierarchy of local officials, backed by the threat of force from nearby garrisons. These 'weekly assessments' were supplemented with a variety of other local taxes and contributions, as well as the hated excise, a sales tax levied on all but the most basic foodstuffs, imposed by Parliament in 1643 and soon copied by the royalists. And on top of these exactions came the confiscation of property, again imposed by both sides. Parliamentarians in royalist-dominated counties, such as Cornwall, had their estates seized between 1643 and 1646. Royalists who lost their estates under the 1643 sequestration ordinance might not recover them for a decade or more, and even then only on payment of substantial fines under a system known as 'composition'.

There were winners as well as losers. Money taken for a garrison, whether through plunder or legitimate taxation, was usually spent in the same town, and goods were bought at markets as well as stolen from houses. Items useful for the war effort, such as uniforms and shoes, were in great demand, and new industries sprang up in unlikely places, including the manufacture of weapons of all kinds in the university city of Oxford. The merchants of the City of London prospered during the war, and certain entrepreneurs, such as Daniel Judd, did very well by supplying ammunition and clothing to Parliament's armies. The cannon foundries of the Kentish Weald and the gunpowder mills on the River Lea in Essex were also much in demand. Dealing in death had never been so profitable.

## Resistance

The taxes imposed by both sides during the first civil war were far higher than anything England had experienced in peacetime. They were bitterly resented, and many people were reluctant to pay. In Hertfordshire, the authorities noted, with some exasperation, at the end of 1644 that 'taxes are so frequent in the country for one thing and another, that when warrants are issued, the returns are often complaints and tears and not moneys as are expected'. Grumbling and passive resistance could easily give way to violence when the actions of the government or its soldiers were seen as unjust and illegal, as in Kent in 1643, when parishioners at Ightham resisted the arrest of their rector, leading to the death of one of the villagers and a revolt led by the local gentry. Those resisting were not royalists – rather, they opposed the illegality of Parliament's policies and the brutality of its henchmen.

A similar mixture of localism and outrage helped to fuel the famous 'clubmen' revolts of 1645. In these uprisings, which spread across the south-west and the Welsh marches, ordinary people armed themselves against the depredations of marauding soldiers, whether Goring's men in Somerset and Devon or the New Model Army on the Dorset–Wiltshire border. The clubmen also put forward sets of demands, usually for peace between the king and Parliament, the disbandment of the rival armies, and, above all, the removal of all soldiers from their local area. These movements were harnessed by ministers, lawyers or gentlemen, and their neutralism compromised by the blandishments of either side, but their existence as a genuine popular element in the wars is revealing.

The kind of interference that riled the protesters in Kent in 1643 and the clubmen of the west in 1645 reappeared with still more force in the winter of 1647–8. The underlying cause may have been a rise in food prices, but there were religious and political elements as well, in favour of the Prayer Book and renewed peace negotiations with the king. In 1648, local unrest was soon hijacked by die-hard royalists, and became twisted to form the series of conflicts, from Kent to South Wales, Penzance to Colchester, known as the second civil war.

## Women

The horrors of war were experienced by men and women alike, but women had additional burdens to bear, and these should not be overlooked. Although they did not play an active role in the field armies of the civil war, many women accompanied their men as camp followers. The Welsh women killed and mutilated as they sheltered with the royalist baggage train after the defeat at Naseby in 1645 were probably mistaken for Irish, and thus liable to suffer unlimited abuse, but this was a rare incident in the wars in England. Rape was also uncommon – or at least seldom reported – and violence towards women tended to be occasional or accidental, as at Wendover in Buckinghamshire in 1642, when Serjeant Wharton's captain forgot his weapon was loaded and 'shot a maid through the head, and she immediately died'. Wharton's men, who had until then enjoyed such pleasures as heavy drinking and trashing the church, were shocked by this, and 'from hence we marched very sadly'. It was evidently more common, and less shameful, to rob women and destroy their homes than to offer them physical violence.

For most women, the war presented problems of a rather different kind, as they were left to continue normal life as best they could, while hoping and praying for their soldier husbands

### SUSAN RODWAY'S LETTER TO HER HUSBAND, WINTER 1643–4

Most dear and loving husband, my King Love,

Remember unto you, hoping that you are in good health, as I am at the writing hereof. My Little Willie have been sick this fortnight. I pray you to come home, if you can come safely. I do marvel that I cannot hear from you as well other neighbours do. I do desire to hear from you as soon as you can. I pray send me word when you do think you shall return. You do not consider I am a lone woman. I thought you would never leave me this long together. So I rest, ever praying for your safe return.

Your loving wife,
Susan Rodway
Ever praying for you till death I depart.

(On the cover) To my very loving husband, Robert Rodway, a train soldier in the red regiment under the command of Captain Warren, deliver this with speed, I pray you.

Source: *Mercurius Aulicus* 52nd week (30 Dec. 1643), p. 745 (We know from other sources that Robert Rodway, a tallow chandler and citizen, survived the war.)

or sons to return safely. Perhaps the most vivid account of a war wife comes from the pen of an ordinary housewife, Susan Rodway, whose husband was a soldier in a London regiment in Sir William Waller's army, engaged in the unsuccessful attack on Basing House in 1643.

The exception to this mostly passive role came when women's homes were in castles or besieged towns, and it was here that they were forced to take a more active part in the civil wars. In the early years of the first civil war, when warfare was local, fluid, and conducted by gentlemen rather than professionals, there were several examples of wives defending strongholds in the absence of their husbands, including the countess of Derby at Lathom in Lancashire, Lady Harley at Brampton Bryan in Herefordshire, and Lady Bankes at Corfe Castle in Dorset. At the siege of Basing House in 1645, the women joined the desperate defence by throwing stones and other missiles at the attacking parliamentarians, and some were killed as a result.

In besieged towns and cities, women as well as men laboured to strengthen defences, the most famous example being that of London, where an eleven-mile circuit of earthen walls, gateways, and bastions was erected from 1642 onwards, with women playing an important role carrying earth and other building materials. There were similar scenes at Gloucester during its siege by royalists in 1643. Less happily, women and children were trapped in the terrible siege of Colchester in 1648, when hunger became a weapon of war. The besieging general, the usually humane Sir Thomas Fairfax, refused to allow civilians to leave the town, and in response his royalist counterpart, the earl of Norwich, forced a large number of women and children out of the gates, leaving them in no man's land, in a 'condition most lamentable, for they could neither go backwards nor forwards, not remain where they were but die suddenly'. This was a shocking breach of ordinary civilian values, and, indeed, of the military code that normally restrained the behaviour of officers.

# Resilience

The horrors of Colchester were very much the exception in England, and it is important not to over-emphasize the social dislocation caused by the civil wars. While the political and religious impact of the conflict was long term, English society seems to have healed itself relatively quickly. The framework of national institutions remained intact throughout the period. The law courts continued to operate. Charles I established his own central courts at Oxford at the end of 1642, and they existed in parallel with their rivals at Westminster. Local courts, the quarter sessions and the assize circuits, became more irregular at the height of the first civil war, but never stopped altogether. Parliament became a permanent institution, passing legislation as well as performing an executive function, and the king instituted his own Parliament at Oxford in 1644–5.

A similar story can be found in the localities. Most towns and cities were not seriously damaged, and normal life was soon resumed. The Nottinghamshire town of Newark may have lost up to a third of its civilian population to disease in nearly four years as a garrison town in the first civil war, but its people were determined not to allow its social order to collapse. A recent study has shown that the corporation made every effort to continue civic life, funding poor relief and the school, and providing its officers with uniforms even at the height of the war. The lower orders joined this struggle to preserve social norms: marriages (including remarriages) increased by 50% in 1644–6, while baptisms had doubled. A similar determination can be seen in the Irish port of Drogheda, infamous as Cromwell's first target in his Irish campaign in September 1649. The scale of civilian casualties is unknown, but the loss of blood did not prevent Drogheda's corporation from meeting on 5 October – within a month of the siege – to choose a new mayor of the staple and other officials, and to arrange for the customs revenues of the port to be farmed out.

Urban areas had the structures to keep going in difficult times, but there is also evidence that rural society was able to return to something close to normality with surprising speed after the end of the conflict. This is especially true of landowning families who risked censure by protecting the property of royalist friends and relatives. A useful case study is that of the Trenchard family of Dorset, who went out of their way to defend the interests of their kinsman Sir John Strangways, a notorious royalist imprisoned by Parliament in the Tower of London. At the end of 1646, Lady

Strangways wrote to her brother, Sir Thomas Trenchard, 'hoping that these distracted times hath not wholly extinguished that natural affection which should be between us', and asking that he and other friends in the House of Commons would speed the release of her husband and the return of his estates on good terms. Sir Thomas promised to help, and by the beginning of 1647 the county committee had agreed to lease back the estate to Lady Strangways pending a decision. With the help of other members of the extended family, Sir John was released from the Tower, and allowed to compound for the return of his lands, in the spring of 1648.

Similar examples can be found in other counties, notably Warwickshire, where Viscount Conway and Fulke Grosvenor were among a number of royalists protected by local parliamentarians, and Yorkshire, where John Lambert and his father-in-law, Sir William Lister, used their influence to protect a number of 'delinquent' families, including Catholics. Perhaps the most extraordinary example is that of Parliament's lord general, the earl of Essex, who, despite his orders that all Irishmen captured by his men should be put to death, went to great lengths to protect the estates of his Irish Catholic half-brother, the earl of Clanricarde, during the first civil war.

This pragmatic desire to heal and settle was not confined to the ruling elite, although examples from lower on the social scale are necessarily more difficult to find. Neutralism was often rooted in a social conservatism that caused individual communities to close ranks against outsiders. As one minister in the midlands confided to his parish register, 'When an uncivil war was being waged throughout the greater part of England, I lived well because I lay low'. The people of one group of Wiltshire villages were also intent on keeping a low profile during the first civil war, agreeing to the demands of either side when necessary, but refusing to make a choice between them. As a result, their pro-royalist ministers survived the war unscathed, remaining undetected until 1646, and it was said of one that 'it was always observed that when at any time the parliament's forces were at Salisbury he never preached, but kept the church doors always shut'.

Others were more accepting. When Captain Francis Freeman and his comrades were quartered in Derbyshire, en route for Scotland, in 1650, he was visited by another soldier (a close friend, nicknamed 'Buckingham' after Charles I's favourite), who 'told me that he had excellent music at his quarters, and invited me to come that night to hear it…I went to his quarters where I found them at supper; the people of the house bid me welcome, and as soon as they had supped, my Buckingham (as I called him) rose from the table, and went to a press-cupboard, where he took out a fife recorder and a cittern, and delivered the recorder to the old man and the cittern to the young man his son, and they played half a dozen lessons, very well in consort'. The soldiers, encouraged by Freeman, responded with songs of their own, and the evening ended very amicably indeed, with 'the woman of the house' later recounting, not unfavourably, that Freeman 'had sung a great many merry songs at her house'. Without the immediate pressures of war, it seems that soldiers and civilians were capable of living cheek by jowl with at least the semblance of harmony.

John Oker, the Gloucester organist, also proved surprisingly resilient. By November 1649, he had returned to Gloucester, and in 1651 he told the commonwealth authorities of some church dues that had not been declared, and was rewarded for his services, partly on the strength of being 'very well affected to the parliament, having been in arms for them'. Even if Oker really had changed sides during the first civil war (as many ordinary soldiers did), this was an extraordinarily audacious claim for a former royalist to make. Nor was this the end of his willingness to adapt and survive. He was admitted freeman of Gloucester in 1654 and a bedesman of the cathedral in 1656, and he received money from the trustees for the maintenance of ministers later in the decade. At the Restoration, he moved back to Wells, where he was appointed cathedral organist in 1661. It had taken nearly twenty years, but John Oker, like so many of his countrymen and women, had finally got back to where he had started.

# 10

# Legacy

After the Restoration, John Oker was not the only one who wanted to turn back the clock, to pretend that the civil wars had not happened. With the accession of Charles II in May 1660, every effort was made to wipe out the history of the previous twenty years. Too many men who now cheered for Charles had been, only a few years before, his implacable enemies. Not least among them was General George Monck, who had started as a royalist soldier, changed sides in the 1640s, and became Cromwell's commander in Scotland. His decision to march south to London in the new year of 1660 had ended any possibility of rule by the army radicals, and put in train the events that led to the return of the king. He had been made duke of Albemarle by the king on his return, and lauded by the court as the godfather of the Restoration, but even he was vulnerable to criticism for his earlier career. Monck was not alone. Edward Montagu – Cromwell's admiral – was made earl of Sandwich in 1660, and remained in command of the Royal Navy. Denzil Holles, one of the five members and a key Presbyterian during the first civil war, was now created Lord Holles.

It was politic not to embark on a public inquiry, still less an exercise in truth and reconciliation. Instead, a select group – the regicides who had signed Charles I's death warrant – became the scapegoats, and a number were subjected to show trials, humiliation, and excruciating deaths, from October 1660 onwards. Some of the key culprits were beyond the reach of Charles II and his henchmen. Oliver Cromwell (who had died in 1658), his son-in-law Henry Ireton (d. 1651), and the president of the council of state, John Bradshaw (d. 1659), were disinterred from their graves in January 1661 and 'executed', with their heads impaled on spikes and exhibited on the roof of Westminster Hall. Soon afterwards, there were further acts of symbolic revenge. The Solemn League and Covenant was publicly burned, and such important parliamentary measures as the attainder of the earl of Strafford or the banning of bishops from sitting in the House of Lords were repealed, and excised from the official records. History was being rewritten.

Despite the royalist airbrush, the Stuarts could not remove the popular memory of the political and religious divisions that had caused civil war and revolution. This was particularly the case after 1662, when the king abandoned attempts to reach a religious settlement with the moderate Presbyterians and enforced instead an exclusively Anglican Church of England, with a prayer book very similar to that used before the civil wars. The whole hierarchy of the church – archbishops, bishops, cathedrals, deans, and chapters – was reintroduced; and anyone who could not accept this was vilified and prosecuted as an enemy of the crown. The failure of the king and his advisers to countenance a compromise destroyed any hope of a new national church, and created a rift between the Established Church and the non-conformists – the Presbyterians, Congregationalists, Baptists, Quakers, and others – which has persisted to this day. Also in 1662, the crown purged urban corporations of any who would not kowtow to the new regime – creating a further layer of hostility. The regicide had been framed by Charles II's government as a sin as well as a crime, but this did not defuse the knowledge that the people had risen against their king and beheaded him.

In October 1662, various farmers and labourers were investigated in Cheshire for speaking out against the new king: 'the young king's head would come to the block as well as his father', said one. The foreign policy disasters later in the decade – and especially the Dutch seizure of royal ships at Chatham in 1667 – brought unfavourable comparisons with the commonwealth period, and especially with Oliver Cromwell. As Samuel Pepys, another former Cromwellian turned royal servant, recorded in his diary: 'Everybody nowadays doth reflect upon Oliver and commend him, so brave things he did, and made all the neighbour princes fear him. While here a prince, come in with all the love and prayers and good liking of his people…hath lost all so soon, that it is a miracle what way any man could devise to lose so much in so little time'.

The civil wars were not forgotten in later decades, especially during the periods of instability and political tension. During the 'Exclusion Crisis' of 1678–81, when many wanted to prevent the Catholic James, duke of York (the future James II) from succeeding his brother, Charles II, to the throne, the spectre of civil war was raised, with some claiming that 'forty-one is come again'. The republican Algernon Sidney identified himself with the regicides and the Good Old Cause when he went to the scaffold in 1683. During the 'Glorious Revolution' of 1688 that removed James II and brought William and Mary to the throne, the civil wars again came to the front of the collective conscious. The securing of the Protestant succession did little to calm political debate.

The totemic importance of the mid-seventeenth century was increased by the publication of rival accounts of the history of the civil wars, notably the *Memoirs* of the regicide Edmund Ludlow (1698–9), which were edited to play down the deep-rooted Puritanism of the original and play up its republicanism, and the *History of the Rebellion* by the royalist earl of Clarendon (formerly Sir Edward Hyde), the first volume of which appeared in 1702. Clarendon helped to create an image of reasonable, constitutional royalism that appealed to the newly emerged Tory party. Sidney and Ludlow, along with John Milton, became the heroes of the

Whig party in England, and their principled opposition to the crown influenced the American Revolutionaries in the 1770s and later.

In the eighteenth century, Oliver Cromwell was a more controversial figure, hated by royalists for killing the king, and by republicans for dissolving the Rump parliament, but the publication of Thomas Carlyle's edition of Cromwell's *Letters and Speeches* in 1845 elevated him into a liberal, non-conformist hero – a process that continued apace until 1899, and the erection of the Thornycroft statue of him immediately outside the Houses of Parliament, at the instigation of Lord Rosebery. Both royalists and parliamentarians inspired the romanticism of the Victorians. In the 1840s, as Carlyle produced a Cromwell attractive to the non-conformists, the Anglicans of the Oxford Movement were rediscovering the Laudian divines, while the high church ritualists of the 1890s adopted the figure of King Charles as a royal martyr, just as Rosebery was planning his statue of Cromwell for Westminster. The two were not unconnected. As Lloyd George reportedly put it in 1899, 'the protector's values and principles are sadly needed today. How he would have dealt with the Ritualists! He would have been worth a wagonload of bishops. How he would have settled the House of Lords!' Numerous paintings show dour puritans and flamboyant cavaliers locked in combat or striking dramatic, soulful poses, from Augustus Leopold Egg's *The Night Before Naseby* of 1859 to William Frederick Yeames' *And When Did You Last See Your Father?*, painted in 1878.

The twentieth century saw no let up in academic interest in the civil wars. The great historians of the turn of the century – S.R. Gardiner and C.H. Firth – led a new, more rigorous approach to the surviving sources for the period, which they considered to be pivotal in the inexorable rise of liberal, parliamentary democracy. They were followed, from the 1930s, by two rival developments. The first was the short-lived attempt to shoehorn Cromwell, in particular, into the role of proto-dictator.

This received a favourable reception on the continent, and it was rumoured that both Hitler and Mussolini had pictures of Cromwell in their offices. The second development was more enduring: the use of Marxist views of history to explain the civil wars in terms of class struggle and economic imperatives. Christopher Hill and others championed this approach, and academic interest moved from the great men and institutions to radical groups, especially the Levellers and Diggers.

In reaction, the 1980s saw the birth of revisionism, and the triumph of the contingent. There were no long-term causes of the civil wars, we were told, only a series of unfortunate events surrounding the inept king, Charles I. Each one of these events was re-examined, and the complexities teased out. The study of the civil wars seemed to suffer death by a thousand qualifications. And so the pendulum swung back again, with post-revisionism again looking for long-term causes, and putting religion back at the centre of the picture.

The impact of these academic fashions on a general public well versed in Victorian romanticism is questionable. To take two examples, Sellar and Yeatman's 1930 comic history of England, *1066 and All That*, caricatured the civil wars being 'the utterly memorable struggle between the Cavaliers (wrong but wromantic) and the Roundheads (right but repulsive)'. The slightly unhinged account of Oliver Cromwell's life by L. du Garde Peach in the Ladybird Book of the same name (first published in 1963) regurgitated all the old myths about the lord protector, accompanied by painted illustrations by John Kenny that reinforced the caricature of the killjoy puritans and the foppish royalists. Similar stereotypes can be seen in the world of film, whether *Witchfinder General* (1968), *Cromwell* (1970), or *To Kill a King* (2003). A trawl of newspapers at the beginning of 2011 revealed a number of civil war-related stories, including the remarkable fact, unearthed by the *Daily Express* (22 February 2011), that Kate Middleton, then soon to become duchess of Cambridge, was descended from

Sir Thomas Fairfax. From such examples, it might be concluded that the general public continues to enjoy its history, but without much reference to the divisions and deliberations of academe.

Having said that, there is no doubt that many people want to know more about the English Civil Wars, and at a much deeper level. Battlefields continue to fascinate, and the wide range of monuments built through the generations are frequently visited. There are memorials at Chalgrove (1643), Lansdown (1643), Dunbar (1650), and Worcester (1651). The battle of Naseby (1645) boasts two monuments. One, the obelisk on Windmill Hill to the south of the battlefield, was erected by the lord of the manor in 1823, and its inscription warns both monarchs and subjects to observe their constitution duties, and not risk 'the horrors of anarchy' once again. The nearby Cromwell monument, unveiled in 1936, is rather different in tone. Presented to the people of Northamptonshire, its purpose is to educate and inspire, reminding locals of 'one of the most important events in the history of your county'. Almost contemporaneous with the latter is the obelisk at Marston Moor in Yorkshire, erected by the liberal politician and founder of the Cromwell Association, Isaac Foot, in 1939. There is something iconic about the battle of Marston Moor on 2 July 1644. It was not the decisive battle of the civil wars, but it was the high water mark of parliamentarian unity, when Independents and Presbyterians, the English and the Scots, came together in a common cause, and this added to its appeal to later generations. As Isaac Foot used to say, 'I judge a man by one thing. Which side would he have liked his ancestors to fight on at Marston Moor?'

Monuments have also become the focus for commemorative events in modern times. The John Hampden Society visits the one at Chalgrove (where Hampden was killed in 1643) annually for a service of remembrance, while the re-enacting societies hold services at the monuments at Naseby in June and Marston Moor in July. The Society of King Charles the Martyr holds its own service at the equestrian statue of the king at the Trafalgar Square end of Whitehall on 30 January each year, and re-enactors from royalist regiments of the King's Army march through Whitehall on the same day. The Cromwell Association arranges a rather different commemoration each year beneath the statue of Oliver Cromwell at Westminster on 3 September – the anniversary of Dunbar, Worcester, and of the lord protector's death – with a wreath being laid at the base of the plinth. The Levellers are remembered every May at Burford in Oxfordshire, where their mutiny was crushed and three ringleaders executed in 1649. Such occasions are attended by enthusiasts for particular causes, by those fascinated by the period, and by others curious to see English eccentricity at its best.

It is particularly interesting that most of these events – like the monuments themselves – are of very recent origins. The Society of King Charles the Martyr was founded not in 1649 or 1660, but in 1894; the Cromwell Association was established in 1937; and the Leveller commemorations at Burford date back to 1975. The civil wars clearly have a deep resonance with many people, especially those interested in military history or the personalities, the heroes and villains, of the past. But are there other, more general, reasons why the period has relevance for us today?

Historians are, with good reason, reluctant to think in terms of the 'relevance' that the past might have for the present, but the continuing legacy of the English Civil War might be considered under a number of headings. Perhaps the most obvious is the impact that the period has on our political institutions and attitudes. This was the period when the power of the monarchy (rather than that of a particular monarch) was questioned for the first time, and, after many attempts to reach a compromise settlement, it was decided to remove the institution altogether. Despite the attempts to return to the status quo after 1660, the fact of the regicide and the republic did not leave the English consciousness, and provides an inspiration today, whether to Marxist historians, those who see the Levellers as proto-socialists, or republicans who argue for the abolition of the monarchy altogether.

In constitutional terms, fear of a return to civil war and inter-regnum doubtless had an impact on the Glorious Revolution of 1688, which saw the establishment of a 'constitutional monarchy' with limits to royal power and (in due course) the development of the office of prime minister, exercising the executive role of the crown. In the centuries since the Restoration, one aim of successive British governments has been to prevent rebellion and revolution from happening again. In this, they have been remarkably successful, although the revolutionary spirit has been successfully exported, to inspire those in America, France, and Russia to seek violent change.

Another lasting political legacy is the alienation of England and Ireland. Hatred of English rule developed over a long time, of course, but the civil wars, and especially the assertion of English right to govern Ireland and to confiscate the estates of the Catho-lic rebels, created a bitter folk memory, which was exploited by Irish nationalists in the nineteenth and twentieth centuries, and created a backlash among the loyalist communities.

The political impact of the civil wars is seldom direct, but it forms an important part of the context within which politics across the British Isles is conducted, and debated, today.

The second area of relevance is perhaps the most important, and that is religion. It has been said that the most enduring legacy of the English Civil War was the disintegration of the Jacobean religious consensus, the collapse of the national church. After the Restoration, the Church of England was only one among an array of options for the faithful, and over the next 150 years or so the Established Church was forced to give ground, allowing non-conformity and even Catholicism to be legal and socially acceptable. As we have seen, much of the interest in characters such as Cromwell during the nineteenth century came from the non-conformist churches, who considered themselves to have a direct spiritual link with the lord protector and his friends. During the twentieth century, this sense of kinship declined – or, rather, the radicals of the seventeenth century became domesticated, and made more socially acceptable. The Quakers of the early 1650s threatened the social and political hierarchy of their day; their twentieth-century counterparts were altogether more civilized. Other parallels are more unsettling. The tendency of modern secular England to ignore religion, or treat it as a matter of personal choice, or social convention, was severely challenged by the events of 11 September 2001. Why are people motivated to do such things? What response do moderates have to religious extremists? The same questions were being asked in January 1649.

Finally, we might consider the relevance of the civil wars to 'heritage' and culture, the shared sense of where we have come from. The civil wars are of particular importance in this respect because they affected almost the whole of England, large areas of Wales, as well as Scotland and (most notoriously) Ireland. There are few localities that lack a historic site – a castle, stately home, battlefield, or ruined town walls – connected with the period, and these are often held in great affection by local people, conscious of the need to connect with the past and to strengthen sometimes fragile modern communities. The challenge is to preserve these sites and present them to the general public in a clear-sighted way, without the myths, misrepresentations, and money concerns of the twenty-first century distorting the picture. The temptation to smooth over the religious and political divisions, to glamorize the conflict, to play up the pageantry, must be resisted. It is only then that the English Civil Wars can be viewed on their own terms, and we can begin to understand the experiences of the very real people caught up in them.

# Timeline

| 1640 | 3 November | Calling of the 'Long Parliament' |
| 1641 | 12 May | Execution of the earl of Strafford |
| | 23 October | Outbreak of Irish rebellion |
| 1642 | January | Attempted arrest of the 'five members'; Charles I leaves London |
| | 5 March | Parliament passes militia ordinance |
| | June | Nineteen Propositions (rejected by the king) |
| | 22 August | King raises his standard at Nottingham |
| | 23 October | Battle of Edgehill, Warwickshire |
| 1643 | Feb.–April | Oxford peace talks |
| | September | Cessation of arms signed in Ireland; Solemn League and Covenant between Parliament and Scots |
| | 20 September | 1st Battle of Newbury, Berkshire |
| 1644 | January | Scottish army enters England |
| | 2 July | Battle of Marston Moor, Yorkshire |
| | Aug.–Sept. | Earl of Essex defeated at Lostwithiel, Cornwall |
| | 27 October | 2nd Battle of Newbury, Berkshire |

| | | |
|---|---|---|
| 1645 | Jan.–Feb. | Uxbridge negotiations |
| | April | Creation of the New Model Army |
| | 14 June | Battle of Naseby, Northamptonshire |
| | October | Storming of Basing House, Hampshire |
| 1646 | 25 June | Surrender of Oxford |
| | July | Newcastle Propositions rejected by king |
| 1647 | January | Scottish army leaves England; king handed over to Parliament |
| | August | New Model Army occupies London |
| | Oct.–Nov. | Putney Debates |
| | December | King signs Engagement with Scots |
| 1648 | May–August | Second civil war |
| | 17–19 August | Battle of Preston, Lancashire |
| | 6 December | Pride's Purge of Parliament |
| 1649 | January | Trial of Charles I |
| | 30 January | Execution of Charles I |
| | February | Abolition of monarchy and House of Lords; appointment of Council of State |
| | 2 August | Battle of Rathmines, Co. Dublin |
| | 11 September | Storming of Drogheda, Co. Louth |
| | 11 October | Storming of Wexford, Co. Wexford |
| 1650 | July | Cromwell marches into Scotland |
| | 3 September | Battle of Dunbar, East Lothian |

| 1651 | 1 January | Charles II crowned at Scone |
| | August | Charles II and Scottish army march into England |
| | 3 September | Battle of Worcester |
| 1653 | 20 April | Cromwell dissolves Rump Parliament |
| | July | 'Barebone's Parliament' sits |
| | December | Creation of the Cromwellian Protectorate |
| 1658 | 3 September | Death of Oliver Cromwell |
| 1659 | April–May | Collapse of Protectorate of Richard Cromwell |
| | May–Oct. | Rump Parliament restored |
| 1660 | January | George Monck crosses the Tweed with his army |
| | 29 May | Restoration of Charles II |

# Further reading

The best general study of this period to appear in recent years is Austin Woolrych, *Britain in Revolution, 1625–1660* (Oxford, Oxford University Press, 2002), while a broader overview is provided in Barry Coward, *The Stuart Age: England, 1603–1714* (4th edn, Pearson, 2012). For a bold, and controversial, reassessment of the civil wars across Britain and Ireland, see David Scott, *Politics and War in the Three Stuart Kingdoms, 1637–49* (Basingstoke, Palgrave, 2004). These three books provide rather different 'takes' on the overall narrative of events, 1642–51. For more detailed examinations of particular political issues, see Robert Ashton, *Counter-Revolution: The Second Civil War and its Origins, 1646–8* (New Haven, Yale University Press, 1994), David Underdown, *Pride's Purge: Politics in the Puritan Revolution* (Oxford, Clarendon Press, 1971), Blair Worden, *The Rump Parliament, 1648–53* (Cambridge, Cambridge University Press, 1974), and Sean Kelsey, *Inventing a Republic: The Political Culture of the English Commonwealth, 1649–1653* (Manchester, Manchester University Press, 1997). Also of value are the essays in four collections: John Morrill, (ed.), *Reactions to the English Civil War, 1642–49* (Basingstoke, Macmillan, 1982); John Adamson, editor, *The English Civil War: Conflicts and Contexts, 1640–49* (Basingstoke, Palgrave, 2009); Jason Peacey, ed., *The Regicides and the Execution of Charles I* (Basingstoke, Palgrave, 2001); and Jason McElligott and David L. Smith, editors, *Royalists and Royalism during the English Civil Wars* (Cambridge, Cambridge University Press, 2007).

The military side of the civil wars has attracted much interest, with varying results. For the experience of the soldiers, the classic book is C.H. Firth, *Cromwell's Army* (4th edn, Fakenham, University Paperbacks, 1962), which should be supplemented by Charles Carlton, *Going to the Wars: The Experience of the English Civil Wars, 1638–1651* (Routledge, 1992) and Barbara Donagan, *War in England, 1642–1649* (Oxford, Oxford University Press, 2008). For military activities more generally, see the essays in John Kenyon and Jane Ohlmeyer, (eds), *The Civil Wars: A Military History of England, Scotland and Ireland, 1638–1660* (Oxford, Oxford University Press, 1998), and for the New Model Army the standard work is Ian Gentles, *The New Model Army in England, Ireland and Scotland, 1645–1653* (Oxford, Blackwell, 1992). The royalist army is considered in Ronald Hutton, *The Royalist War Effort, 1642–1646* (2nd edn, London, Routledge, 1999). A useful overview of the battles and campaigns is provided in Malcolm Wanklyn, *The Warrior Generals: Winning the British Civil Wars* (New Haven, Yale University Press, 2010), and reliable studies of individual commanders include Alan Marshall, *Oliver Cromwell, Soldier: The Military Life of a Revolutionary at War* (London, Brassey's, 2004) and Andrew Hopper, *'Black Tom': Sir Thomas Fairfax and the English Revolution* (Manchester, Manchester University Press, 2007).

The political thinking of the period has been much studied, but there is little that is accessible to the general reader. Perhaps the best starting points are the essays by Malcolm Smuts and J.C. Davis on political thought before and during the civil wars in Barry Coward, (ed.), *A Companion to Stuart Britain* (Oxford, Wiley-Blackwell, 2003). For the army debates in the later 1640s, see Austin Woolrych, *Soldiers and Statesmen: The General Council of the Army and its Debates, 1647–1648* (Oxford, Clarendon Press, 1987), and for the development of republican ideas, see Blair Worden, *Literature and Politics in Cromwellian England: John Milton, Andrew Marvell, Marchamont Nedham* (Oxford, Oxford University Press, 2007). A sound introduction to print culture can be found in Nigel Smith, *Literature and Revolution in England,*

*1640–1660* (New Haven, Yale University Press, 1994). For more detailed discussion of propaganda, see Kevin Sharpe, *Image Wars: Promoting Kings and Commonwealths in England, 1603–1660* (New Haven, Yale University Press, 2010) and Jason Peacey, *Politicians and Pamphleteers: Propaganda During the English Civil Wars and Interregnum* (Aldershot, Ashgate, 2004).

The experience of the Church of England during the war years is explored in three essays: John Morrill, 'The Church in England, 1642–9', in Morrill (ed.), *Reactions to the English Civil War*; Judith Maltby, 'Suffering and Surviving: The Civil Wars, the Commonwealth and the Formation of "Anglicanism"', in Christopher Durston and Judith Maltby, (eds), *Religion in Revolutionary England* (Manchester, Manchester University Press, 2006); and Anthony Milton, 'Anglicanism and Royalism in the 1640s', in Adamson, *The English Civil War*. The classic work on radical religion is Christopher Hill, *The World Turned Upside Down: Radical Ideas During the English Revolution* (Harmondsworth, Penguin, 1975), and for a more recent discussion of the same, see the essays in Durston and Maltby, *Religion in Revolutionary England*. For mainstream Puritanism, see Christopher Durston and Jacqueline Eales, *The Culture of English Puritanism, 1560–1700* (Basingstoke, Macmillan, 1996).

The civilian experience of war is covered in Carlton, *Going to the Wars*. For the wider context, see also John Morrill, *Revolt in the Provinces: The People of England and the Tragedies of War* (2nd edn, London, Longman, 1999). For the material damage caused by war, see Stephen Porter, *Destruction in the English Civil Wars* (Stroud, Alan Sutton, 1994). Fascinating case studies are provided by David Underdown, *Fire from Heaven: Life in an English Town in the Seventeenth Century* (Hammersmith, Fontana, 1993) and Stuart B. Jennings, *'These Uncertaine Tymes': Newark and the Civilian Experience of the Civil Wars, 1640–1660* (Nottingham, Nottinghamshire County Council, 2009). For a flavour of life as lived by ordinary people during the period, see Margaret Spufford, *Small*

*Books and Pleasant Histories: Popular Fiction and its Readership in Seventeenth-Century England* (Cambridge, Cambridge University Press, 1981); Paul S. Seaver, *Wallington's World: A Puritan Artisan in Seventeenth-Century London* (London, Methuen, 1985); and Christopher Marsh, *Music and Society in Early Modern England* (Cambridge, Cambridge University Press, 2010). For insights into the lives of the better-off, see Linda Levy Peck, *Consuming Splendor: Society and Culture in Seventeenth-Century England* (Cambridge, Cambridge University Press, 2005) and Keith Thomas, *The Ends of Life: Roads to Fulfilment in Early Modern England* (Oxford, Oxford University Press, 2009).

# Index